The Science of Computing

quantum scientific publishing

The Science of Computing

Sriram Iyengar, PhD

quantum scientific publishing

The Science of Computing

ISBN-13: 978-1482328677
ISBN-10: 1482328674

Published by quantum scientific publishing

Pittsburgh, PA | Copyright © 2013

Cover design by Scott Sheariss

QUANTUM
SCIENTIFIC
PUBLISHING

For Jahnavi

Table of Contents

Unit Three

Appendix

Unit One

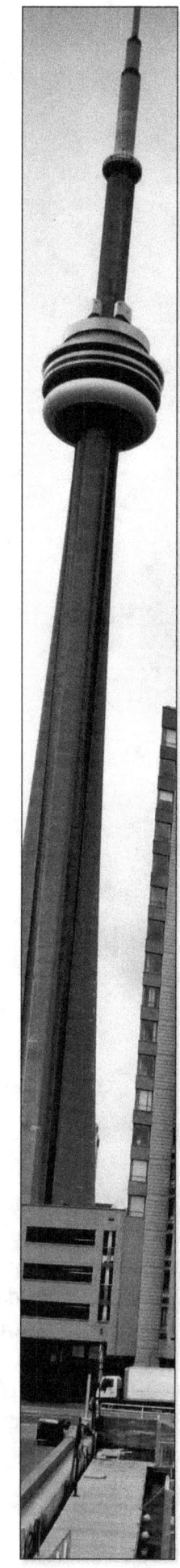

Section 1.1 – Stonehenge and its Significance in the Science of Computing

Section Objective:

- Understand the significance of Stonehenge in the science of computing, and analyze its impact on future technologies

What is Stonehenge?

About 90 miles west of London, England, in a large flat area called Salisbury Plain there is a collection of stone monoliths arranged in a circle. This circle contains additional monoliths, some forming an inner circle, and others in a linear pattern. The upright stones are called sarsens. Each is about 10 feet tall and weighs 26 to 50 tons. Some pairs of upright stones support additional stones laid horizontally across their tops. The diameter of the outermost circle is about 110 meters. Just within the outermost circle is a ring of 56 small pits called Aubrey holes.

A picture of Stonehenge.

Origins

Stonehenge has been dated to be anywhere between 3000 to 5000 years old. The sarsens came from a quarry 20 miles away. Some of the inner stones, called bluestones, weigh 4 tons each and are believed to have come from the mountains in Wales, 240 miles away. It is clear that strenuous prolonged effort must have been involved in cutting the stones, dragging them, or floating them down rivers, for considerable distances, digging deep foundation ditches, installing the vertical stones, making sure they were of uniform height and then lifting the heavy stones (6 tons each) on top of the vertical ones. There are believed to be three or four phases of construction of the entire structure, from about 3100 BC to about 1600 BC. Knowing that all of this amazing construction was done without the aid of any modern construction equipment only adds to the wonderment people feel when they visit.

An aerial view of a Stonehenge replica.

The people who built Stonehenge were early (Neolithic period) inhabitants of England who left no written records or history. Many theories have been proposed, including some involving Merlin, a magician in the court of King Arthur, Druidical priests, help from aliens, a race of giants, and so on.

Function

Given the enormous efforts needed to construct it, the peoples who built Stonehenge must have had a compelling reason to do so. Many speculations have been devised in this regard.

One of these theories claims that Stonehenge is some kind of predictive calendar, enabling prediction of lunar eclipses, and track the movement of important constellations, equinoxes, and similar celestial phenomena. It has been suggested that the ancients used Stonehenge as a calculator for the date of events such as lunar eclipses by moving a small number of (3 to 6) stones around and depositing them in a like number of the 56 Aubrey holes. By shifting the stones in sequence at each winter solstice, lunar events of that year could be predicted. This view has some credibility because astronomy played a much more immediate role in the lives of ancient peoples than to us. For one thing, there was much less light pollution, and nights were truly dark, enabling the moon and the stars to be much more visible than they are today to most humans. Some also believe that agricultural events such as planting and harvesting were set according to astronomical events.

An interesting viewpoint from medicine is that Stonehenge is a symbolic representation of female anatomy and therefore a tribute to the Earth Mother Goddess as a celebration of fertility.

Another theory suggests that Stonehenge is a burial location for rulers. Indeed some human remains have been found and there is evidence of a large city not too far away. This would make the function of Stonehenge similar to the reason why the pyramids in Egypt and Latin America were constructed.

Since the function of Stonehenge has never been conclusively determined it has had no practical impact on computing. However, if someone does establish conclusively that it was some kind of calculator, then the sociological implication is that computation has been an important concern and activity since the early dawn of humankind.

Concept Reinforcement:

1. Looking at the diagram and pictures of Stonehenge, what features suggest its possible use as an astronomical calendar or calculator?

2. Describe a sarsen.

3. Explain the potential significance of Stonehenge on future understanding of human computational history.

Section 1.2 – The Abacus

Section Objective:

- Understand the significance of he Abacus on the science of computing, and analyze its impact on future technologies

What is the Abacus ?

The Abacus is a mechanical device used for counting and to perform basic arithmetic operations, mostly addition/subtraction. It is a frame containing wires or rods on which beads are strung. Arithmetical operations are performed by moving the beads on the wires in specific ways. It is still in use in many parts of Asia.

A close-up of a wooden abacus.

Origins

In one form or the other many cultures, dating back to 2700 BC (in Sumeria), have used mechanical devices to speed up and enhance the accuracy of performing arithmetic operations. As commerce and trade increased in importance to the well-being of communities, there was increasing need to do arithmetic, and hence a need for devices to aid in doing counting and arithmetic.

The earliest such devices were counting boards consisting of a slab of wood (or stone or metal) with either painted lines or grooves within which pebbles could be moved. The location of the pebbles within the rows indicated the value of a number.

Counting boards and earlier kinds of abaci were used by Greeks, Romans, Persians, Indians and other civilizations. The Chinese abacus, suanpan, is believed to have originated in the 14th century and gave rise to the Japanese abacus (Soroban) in the 1600s.

The Chinese abacus, as can be seen in the figure, consists of an upper part (heaven) and a lower part (earth) separated by a beam. The wires on the upper part contain only two beads, each having a value of 5 while those in the lower contain 5 beads each having a value of 1. Beads are moved up or down mostly using the thumb and index finger. Numbers are read from left to right with the rightmost wire corresponding to the lowest place value and the leftmost to the highest. So, if the operator wanted to designate the 3rd rod from the right as the units place, the two on the right would represent 2 decimal places.

To store a number then will consist of moving beads. The empty position (in which no numbers have been entered) corresponds to that in which the heaven beads are next to the topmost frame and the earth beads to the bottom frame. In other words, both sets of beads are away from the beam.

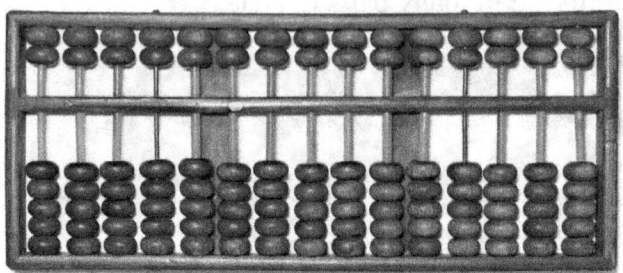

A cleared Chinese abacus.

Let us assume that there are no decimals. Then, the rightmost rod corresponds to the 1s place. To enter the number 5384 into the abacus, we do the following steps that must be done in sequence from left to right:

- On the 4th rod move one heaven bead to the beam

- on the 3rd from the right move three earth beads to the beam

- on the 2nd from the right, move one heaven bead to the beam and 3 earth ones to the beam

- Finally, on the rightmost rod move 4 earth beads towards the beam

- Now, to add the number 15 to 5384 you can simply move one heaven bead in the rightmost rod towards the beam, and one earth bead in the 2nd rightmost rod towards the beam and read off the result from left to right as 5399. A similar procedure is used to add larger numbers; one has to take care of the carries carefully.

Subtraction is accomplished by moving beads away from the beam. Multiplication and division can also be done in more complicated moves.

It is important to note that the abacus is not a calculator. It is a mechanical cognitive aid that helps people count numbers and do simple arithmetic.

As such it really hasn't had much impact on computer science. However, it has certainly reinforced the notion that arithmetic can be automated using mechanical devices. From a commercial point of view, for centuries it has helped shopkeepers in Asia perform transactions with great speed and accuracy.

Concept Reinforcement:

1. On the Chinese abacus shown, how will you enter the number 4265.832?

2. How will you subtract 634.792 from that number?

3. Can the abacus store negative numbers?

Section 1.3 – The Pascaline Calculator

Section Objective:

- Understand the significance of the Pascaline Calculator on the science of computing, and analyze its impact on future technologies

What is the Pascaline Calculator?

The Pascaline computer was one of the first mechanical calculating machines. It was invented in 1642 by a 21-year old French mathematical genius named Blaise Pascal. Pascal's father was a tax collector in the town of Rouen, and Pascal invented his machine to help his father keep track of accounts.

A picture of a pascaline calculator.

Several versions of the Pascaline were built, capable of having 5 to 8 digits. From the above picture you can see that each sprocketed wheel corresponds to one digit and there are ten sprocket holes in each of the wheels. There is a metal stop bar below each wheel. Numbers can be entered by inserting a little stick into the sprocket home corresponding to the desired digit and rotating clockwise till the stop bar is reached. The complete number then shows up in the top pane. To add two numbers, the user entered them in succession and the sum would be displayed on the top bar.

The Pascaline calculator's internal workings are based on constructing a series of gear wheels, one each for the units, tens, hundreds, etc, places and are located under the sprocketed wheels. The basic principle is to construct the gears in such a way that ten rotations of a gear are needed to make the next gear (corresponding to the next higher place) rotate once. Pascal devised an intricate and delicate system of levers to make sure that the carries work correctly and that the final result was visible in the top read-out panel.

The Pascaline was designed to perform only addition. Subtraction could be performed by a clever trick (still used today in modern computers, but implemented electronically) called nines-complement. The nines- complement of any number is obtained by subtracting that number from as many nines as there are digits in that number. So, the nines-complement of 5642 is $9999 - 5642 = 4357$. This is easy subtraction since there are no borrows. Now suppose you want to subtract the number 76 from the number 3698, using the Pascaline.

This is equivalent to computing $3698 + (99 - 76) + 1 - 100.$, which reduces to $3698 + 22 + 1 - 100$. Note that the nines-complement representation of the number 76 is 22. After doing the three additions we get $3721 - 100 = 3621$.

To do a subtraction the following steps are needed:

- Mentally, or using pencil and paper, convert the number to the right of the minus sign into nines complement.

- Add one to it (again easy to do mentally)

- Now add the result to the number on the left of the minus sign using the Pascaline

- Subtract the appropriate power of 10 from the result. Here appropriate means that if the number of digits in the original number to the right of the minus sign is 1, then subtract 10, if 2, subtract 100 and so on.

Multiplications could be performed by converting into a series of additions and division by a series of subtractions. In both cases, the operator of the Pascaline had to make additional written and mental notes to keep track of the operations.

Significance, Impact on Future Technologies

About 50 Pascalines were built but due to their delicate mechanism they needed frequent repair and the invention never came into widespread use. In spite of this, the Pascalines inspired other inventors, including Gottfried Leibniz (a co-inventor of the Calculus) to develop mechanical calculating machines. Eventually, reliable mechanical calculating machines were developed and remained in use until the advent of electronic calculators in the 1950s.

Concept Reinforcement:

1. What is the nines-complement representation of 69432?

2. Rewrite 734 x 49 as a series of additions.

3. Describe a Pascaline calculator and its significance.

Section 1.4 – The Difference and Analytical Engines

Section Objective:

- Understand the significance of The Difference and Analytical Engines on the science of computing, and analyze its impact on future technologies

What were The Difference and Analytical Engines?

The difference and analytical engines (DE and AE) were two mechanical computers that were conceived, but never actually completed, by an amazing British mathematician, engineer and inventor called Charles Babbage, in the UK. Babbage eventually became the Lucasian Professor of Mathematics at Cambridge University, a position occupied by Isaac Newton, and currently by Stephen Hawking. The DE was primarily intended to simplify the calculation of mathematical tables like tables of logarithms, while the AE had all the elements of modern computers.

Origins

Babbage developed these machines because there were increasing demands for mathematical calculations for navigation, accounting, and similar purposes, and also because of the sheer drudgery involved in calculation. During his time, government and industry hired people (known as computers because they performed computations) to perform calculations by hand. The resulting work was tedious, took a lot of time, and had high error rates. He saw that these calculations could be automated by mechanical means and decided to first construct the DE with supporting funds from the government. While this was in progress he realized that while the DE was merely a calculator, he could develop a more general purpose computer, the Analytical Engine.

Both of these were mechanical machines consisting of wheels, gears, cranks, shafts and other moving parts. To set them in continuous motion Babbage proposed using an attached steam engine

Babbage actually designed two versions of the DE, now called DE1 and DE2. These machines were not completed in Charles Babbage's lifetime. One reason given is that he was never satisfied and would constantly come up with must-have improvements until the government, seeing no progress, stopped giving him any more money. Recently, however, working from his original drawings, a few working versions of the DE have been completed. The latest is located in the computer history museum in Mountain View, California. It weighs 5 tons and is operated by turning a crank. It reaches the functionality of a simple pocket calculator while providing precision up to 31 decimal digits.

A photo of a replica difference engine courtesy of Steinsky.

The mathematical basis of the DE is as follows. From calculus, it turns out that important mathematical functions like logarithms, sines, cosines etc can be represented as a series of polynomials. A polynomial in general looks like this:

$$p(x) = C_0 + C_1 x + C_2 x^2 + ... + C_n x^n$$

Here the Cs are numerical coefficients, and n is an integer called the degree of the polynomial.

Computing polynomials, for any value of x, needs multiplication. However, Isaac Newton had discovered the method of divided differences that enabled calculation of polynomials of degree less than 3 into a series of subtractions starting from an accurate initial value of the desired polynomial. The name Difference engine stems from its use of this technique.

The DE consists of several columns, each of which is able to store one number. The initial value of the polynomial is stored in the first column and thereafter the machine computes finite differences and adds them up to produce values of the polynomial for desired values of x.

Work on a prototype of the DE began in 1822 but was never completed.

The Analytical Engine

The Analytical Engines uses as input a series of punched cards and performs whatever calculation is encoded in the punched cards. Thus, unlike the DE, that could perform only the fixed kinds of calculations (computation of polynomials) that were embedded in its mechanical design and construction, the AE could theoretically perform any kind of computation. In modern terms, we would say that the punched cards contain a program, and the AE is a general purpose computer. In fact, Babbage envisioned his AE having a store for numbers (memory), and a mill for doing arithmetical operations including comparisons (arithmetic unit). A form of Central processing unit was also designed consisting of rotating barrels with peg markers inside. All of these features put together in mechanical form could (theoretically) enable most functions of modern computers including branching (checking the value of a quantity and performing different computational steps depending on the value), iteration (repeating steps), looping (returning to a previous step).

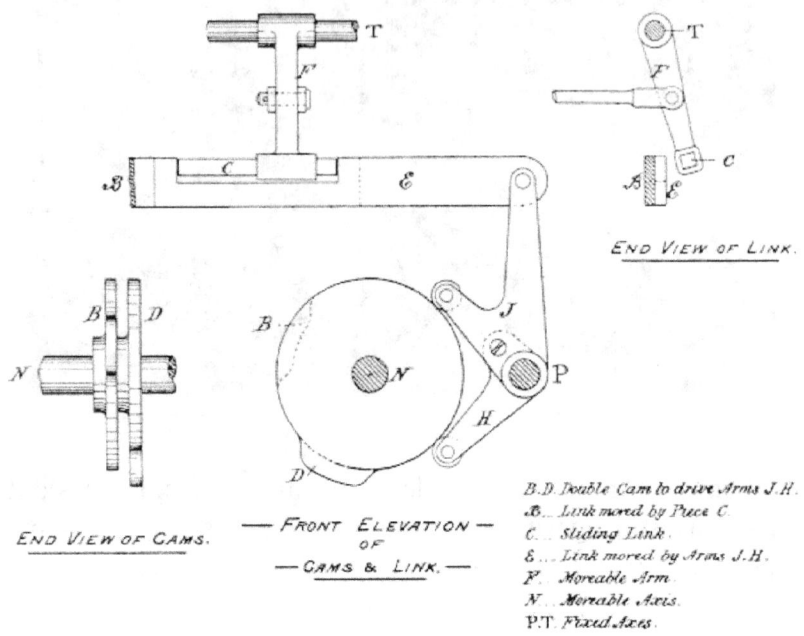

A sketch of an analytical engine.

Babbage's AE concept fascinated an accomplished mathematician, the Countess of Lovelace, Augusta Ada Byron King, daughter of the poet Charles Byron, who achieved rock star status and notoriety in the early 1800s. Applying the AE's concepts in 1842 – 1843 she developed a method to calculate a certain series of numbers called Bernouilli numbers. For this reason she is honored as the first ever computer programmer.

The punched cards themselves have an interesting origin. They were invented in 1801 by Joseph Jacquard in France to automate the weaving of designs by mechanical looms. The desired pattern was encoded into stiff cardboard by punching holes at specified locations in rows on the card. A series of cards thus enabled the loom to be programmed to produce desired patterns.

The AE was designed around 1849 but Babbage could not get funding for its construction and to date none has been built.

Significance, Impact on Future Technologies

Charles Babbage's ideas and writings were known to several mathematicians during his time and disseminated in the UK, Europe, and the USA. It is possible that Alan Turing, Vannevar Bush, and other pioneers of computing in the mid 20th century had read his work and were influenced by it. The DE and AE are significant in the history of computing but any direct impact on modern computing is open to question.

Concept Reinforcement:

1. What are the inherent limitations of mechanical computers as opposed to electronic computers.

2. With respect to functionality what is a significant advance of the AE over the DE?

Section 1.5 – The Tabulating Machine

Section Objective:

- Understand the significance of the tabulating machine on the science of computing, and analyze its impact on future technologies

What was the tabulating machine?

The tabulating machine (TM) was an electro-mechanical machine designed to help collect, count, and assemble statistics . This entire process is called Tabulation (i.e., converting into tables of results).The TM was invented by an American statistician and engineer, Herman Hollerith.

Origins

The US constitution mandates a general census of the entire population every 10 years.. Hollerith had worked in the census of 1880 and found the process laborious and error-prone. Further, from 1880 to 1890 a wave of immigration caused a large rise in the population of the USA and it was predicted that results from the constitutionally mandated 1890 census would take 13 years to tabulate. Hollerith's system, which included the use of punched cards as well as his famous tabulating and sorting machines, is said to have reduced that time very drastically, to a matter of months.

Details

Hollerith's system included the use of punched cards, 7.375" by 3.25" in size. The use of card to control a machine had been pioneered by the French inventor Jacquard. Hollerith's cards were encoded by punching holes at specific locations according to the type of data (race, age, sex etc). Cards were then fed into the tabulating machine one at a time. As it was fed into the machine each card went underneath a collection of spring-loaded metal wires and over a tray filled with little pools of mercury, an electrical conductor. The wires could not penetrate solid areas of paper but when they encountered a hole, the wire made contact with the mercury pool below. This competed a circuit and triggered a counter in the TM.

A picture of a tabulating machine from 1890.

The TM was quite a sophisticated machine, containing sets of counters and also a collection of switches that instructed the TM to look for cards with desired values of race, profession, etc, and sort cards that met these containers into separate bins.

Significance

The TM was the very first accurate and reliable statistical data collection machine. Very rapidly it automated and simplified the hitherto labor-intensive, tedious, and error-prone process of counting and collating vast amounts of data. Many businesses and government organizations realized that they now had a means of obtaining meaningful information from raw data. Statistical analysis of large quantities of data was enabled by the TM and related technologies. Information processing took a giant leap forward.

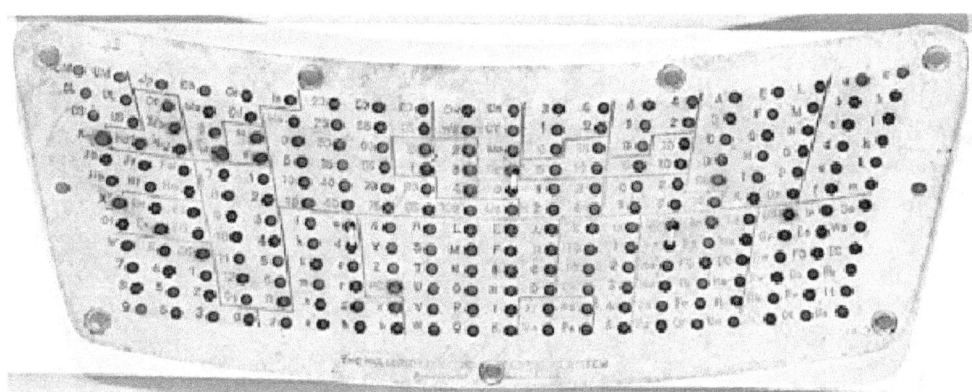

A picture of a keypunch machine.

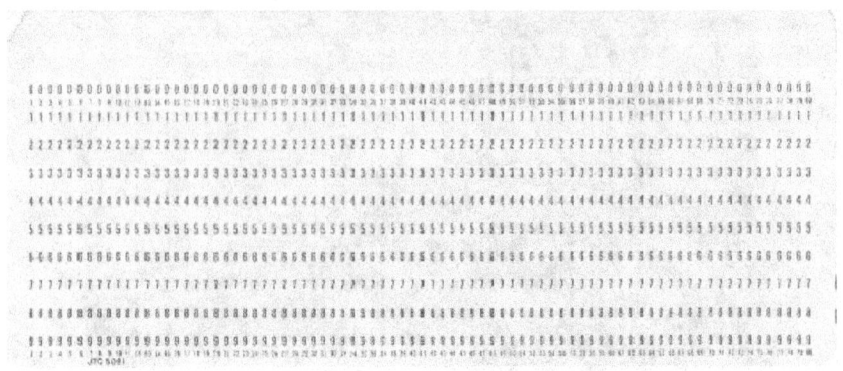

A picture of a punched out card.

Impact on Future Technologies

The TM and its successors have had an enormous impact on computing technologies. The technology of using punched cards, together with keypunch machines, card readers, duplicators and the like remained ubiquitous until the late 1980s.

But perhaps the biggest impact on technology of the TM arose after Herman Hollerith formed the Tabulating Machines Company in 1896. This successful company merged with several others and became the Computing Tabulating Recording Corporation (CTR) in 1911. And in 1924 this became a company that was synonymous with computing for many decades, IBM.

The enormous worldwide success of IBM was, in large part because it gave great support and encouragement to research and development in computer science, leading to a host of inventions such as the magnetic disk, the PL-1 language, relational database technology, and hundreds of others. In this way, Herman Hollerith's Tabulating machine led directly to modern computing.

Concept Reinforcement:

1. How did the TM improve the process of collecting statistical information?

2. Explain the role of the punched card in Holleith's system.

Section 1.6 – Binary Representation

Section Objective:

- Understand the significance binary representation had on the science of computing, and analyze its impact on future technologies

What is the Binary representation?

The word 'binary' signifies a pair of objects. The *binary representation* of numbers is a way of using just two symbols, typically 0 and 1, to represent any whole number. In contrast, the decimal (deci is a prefix for 10 in Latin) system that we commonly use is based on 10 symbols, 0, 1, 2, 3, 4, 5, 6, 7, 8, 9. In the binary system, the decimal number 8 can be written as 110, the decimal number 9 as 111, and so on. We could use any two distinct symbols such as % and @, or True and False; the use of 0 and 1 just happens to be traditional. The 0 and 1 symbols typically used are also called the *binary digits* just as the 10 symbols used in the decimal system are also called *decimal digits*. Any mathematical operation that can be done on decimal numbers can also be done on binary numbers. Also, the binary representation can be easily extended to include not just whole numbers but also fractions and negative numbers.

While this fact had been known for a long time, it was regarded merely as a numeric curiosity. However, with the advent of modern computing in the middle of the twentieth century, the binary representation of numbers became extremely significant and useful. In fact, without the binary representation, the huge advances made by computer science in the last 50 years would not have been possible, and computers as we know them would not exist.

Significance

The reason is that modern computers are *digital* computers. This means that they are designed to speedily and easily store and perform operations on numbers. As opposed to the abacus or to Stonehenge, modern computers are electronic devices. Electronics engineers are very good at building circuits that can exist in one of only two possible states at a time, and the circuits can be made to easily flip-flop from one state to the other by means of a low voltage electronic signal. The special name for these circuits is *logic circuits*. Further, any binary arithmetic operation can be performed by special electronic circuits.

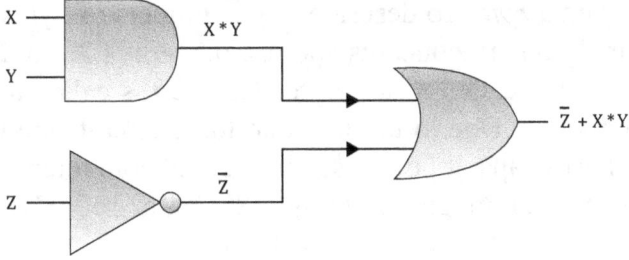

Logic circuit example for implementing the Boolean formula shown at the right of the picture . Here X, Y, and Z are either 0 or 1. The circuit multiplies X and Y, takes the complement of Z and then adds these together.

While a single one of these circuits can only represent the numbers 0 or 1, by stringing several of these circuits together we can store larger and larger numbers. For example, if 8 such circuits are strung together then the smallest number it can store is 00000000 and the largest is 11111111, corresponding to decimal 0 and decimal 255 respectively. Such logic circuits are used to create a computer's *Random Access Memory* (RAM) and more sophisticated combinations of these can do arithmetic operations like addition, subtraction, multiplication, and so on. In a computer, the collection of circuits that does arithmetic is called the *Arithmetic Logic Unit* (ALU).

So far, we have talked about the binary representation of numbers. Computer scientists realized that even alphabetic letters (both upper and lower case) and special symbols such as $ and % can be represented using the binary representation. Therefore, an industry group created the ASCII (American Standards Code for Information Interchange) system in which it was declared that each of the common alphabetic, numeric and special symbols would require a byte and each was assigned a particular pattern of 0s and 1s. Thus the ASCII representation of the letter uppercase 'S' is 01010011 and that for lowercase 's' is 01110011. By means of this system, the binary representation enabled computers to 'understand' not just numbers, but also letters and words.

The Binary Way to Store Information

As you may have noticed, when a computer is shut off, it loses all the information in its RAM. The reason is that logic circuits typically retain their state only so long as electricity is flowing. Once the current is shut off a logic circuit 'forgets' whether it was a 1 or a 0 and if the current comes back will not remember which one it was when switched off. To enable long-term storage of information, engineers also created magnetic devices in which the magnetic surface consists of tiny sections, each of which can exist in only one of two magnetic states. One state can be identified as 0 and the other as 1. An electromagnetic 'pen' can write and read 1s and 0s on the surface and the surface can store the 'written' information as long as needed. These magnetic storage devices are often called *disk drives* since the magnetic surface is a disk kept rotating by a motor when in use. While they can retain information even when they are turned off, reading and writing information from such magnetic storage is very slow compared to the logic circuits comprising RAM. On the other hand magnetic storage is much cheaper to make compared to fast logic circuits. Hence, the RAM 'capacity' of typical computers is much less than the attached magnetic storage.

The storage capacity of RAM, or disk drives, is measured as the amount of binary numbers it can hold. A binary circuit that can be in one of only two states is called a *bit,* and a collection of 8 of these is called a *byte*. To describe large numbers of bytes, computer scientists and engineers again apply binary concepts and use powers of 2. So, 2^{10} (corresponding to 1024 in decimal notation) is called a KiloByte (KB), 2^{20} is called a megabyte (MB), 2^{30} is a gigabyte (GB) and so on. Due to the fact that logic circuits are more expensive than magnetic storage, the RAM capacity of most commercial computers is much less (say 512 MB or 1GB) compared to their magnetic storage (80GB, or 160 GB).

Of course, computers do much more than just do operations on numbers and letters. Nowadays computers show and manipulate movies, pictures, words, and play music. This is because sophisticated mathematics, implemented in complicated electronic circuits, convert these media into binary numbers and back again. In other words, all forms of information can be converted into binary numbers, processed in desired ways, and the results can again be converted back into the original type of information.

Impact on Future Technologies

As we have seen, the binary representation of numbers has played a very major role in the spectacular development of computing in the last 50 years. Because it is so simple, it is easy to construct fast electronic circuits based on binary logic to perform mathematical operations. Magnetic storage based on binary states has been developed that can hold vast troves of information. Recently, *Flash* storage, a new kind of information storage based on electronic (rather than magnetic) circuits has become very popular. This technology also uses logic circuits based on binary representation of numbers.

Scientists are researching electro-magnetic technologies that can enable a device to be in one of more than two states. If a circuit of the same physical size as a present day logic circuit could be in 3 or more states then it can hold much more information than a binary circuit. However, as of today none of these can operate as reliably, or manufactured as easily as binary logic circuits. Thus, it appears that the binary representation is here to stay for many more years.

Concept Reinforcement:

1. Describe why binary numbers are important to modern computing technology.

2. Explain how the implementation of ASCII standards supported the use of computers for applications requiring letters and special symbols.

3. Discuss your thoughts on the future of computing technology. What do you think the next technologies will be able to do?

Section 1.7 – The Mark 1 Computer

Section Objective:

- Understand the significance of the Mark 1 on the science of computing, and analyze its impact on future technologies

What was the Mark 1 Computer?

There were actually two Mark 1 computers. The first was a research prototype built at the Department of Electrical Engineering in the University of Manchester, England in 1949. Based on the successful operation of this machine, a commercial version was developed by Ferranti, a company also located in Manchester in 1951. These are called the Manchester Mark 1 (MM1) and the Ferranti Mark 1 (FM1) respectively. The Ferranti Mark 1 improved upon the Manchester Mark 1 but did not add any revolutionary new features.

In the following we shall first focus on the MM1 and then describe the improvements incorporated in the FM1.

A picture of the Manchester Mark I.

The Manchester Mark 1

The MM1 is notable because it had all the basic elements of modern computers. Many regard it as the first computer to be a true stored-program computer. Unlike other contemporary machines such as the ENIAC that had to be 'programmed' by physically throwing switches and reconnecting cables, the MM1 was able to load programs and data into a memory store and perform operations on the data using the program instructions. This corresponds to Random Access Memory (RAM), also known as main memory, in modern computers. While modern RAM is built using semiconductor logic circuitry, the MM1 used an interesting invention called the Williams-Kilburn tube. This is a cathode ray tube in which a heated element at one end shoots electrons down the length of the tube to the other end onto a glass screen coated with a phosphor. The location on the screen is set by directing the electron beam using electromagnets surrounding the length of the tube. It turns out that a lit up dot on the screen is slightly positively charged compared to the area around it which is slightly negatively charged. This charge difference lasts a fraction of a second and can be sensed by circuitry on the screen. By continually refreshing these dots memory is created. The MM1's two tubes could each hold 64 row of 40 points each, resulting in 2560 bits, or 320 bytes in each tube.

The MM1 also included secondary storage in the form of drum memory. Drum memory had been invented in 1932 by an Austrian, Gustav Tauschek. Here, the sides of a metallic drum were coated with a magnetic material and a column of read-write heads runs up and down the main axis of the drum. The drum rotates and the read/write heads write or read data at specific locations according to inputs coming either from the computer or from paper tape.

The logic system (Central Processing Unit) of the MM1 used 4,200 vacuum tubes to implement arithmetic and logical operations. The MM1 could perform one instruction every 1,800 micro-seconds. Output was typically written out to paper tape or the magnetic drums. Another pioneering innovation of the MM1 was the use of a special memory called an index register. The use of this index register enabled more complex programs that operate upon arrays of data.

Among the remarkable people who worked on the MM1 team were mathematicians Alan Turing, regarded as the father of modern computing, and also a couple, Conway and Mary Berners-Lee whose son Tim invented the world wide web. The first program executed by the MM1 was run in April 1949 and it concerned arithmetic of prime numbers.

The Ferranti Mark 1

The MM1 was a research prototype but its success led to the Ferranti Mark 1 (FM1) intended for commercial use. The engineers at Ferranti were able to improve on the MM1 in several ways, increasing the speed of addition to 1,200 microseconds and multiplication to 2,160 microseconds. Main memory was still based on Williams-Kilburn tubes, used for programs, data, and temporary storage used by the CPU such as accumulators and registers.

Significance and Impact on Future Technologies

Most, if not all components of modern computers can be traced back to the Mark 1 computers. As the first stored program computer it was an empirical demonstration of the Universal Turing Machine conjectured mathematically by Alan Turing. Their speed, remarkable for the time, showed how computing could help solve important scientific and mathematical problems. The fact that they could be programmed to run a diverse array of problems inspired the development of one of the first programming languages, called Autocode, in the 1950s.

For all these reasons the Mark 1's have had great impact on the development of computing.

Concept Reinforcement:

1. What does the drum memory of the MM1 computers correspond to in modern computers?

2. Explain the functions of the Williams-Kilburn tubes in the MM1 computers.

3. Explain some benefits of store program computers over those 'programmed' by reconfiguring hardware.

Section 1.8 – The Turing Machine

Section Objective:

- Understand the significance the Turing machine had on the science of computing, and analyze its impact on future technologies

What is the Turing Machine?

Despite its name, the Turing Machine is not silicon and metal hardware. It is a mathematical idealization of computing (and computers) named after its creator, *Alan Turing* (1912 – 1954), a British mathematical genius. During the Second World War Alan Turing was a key member of a team of mathematicians that helped the British break the code created by Enigma, a device used by the Germans for keeping their military communications secret. Earlier, in the 1930s, he had become interested in developing a model of computation that could apply to any conceivable kind of computer. In other words, he wanted to understand the mathematical basis of computation itself. For this reason, the formulation of the Turing machine is regarded as the birth of computer science.

Over the years mathematicians have develop many variations of the Turing Machine. Here, a simple one is described.

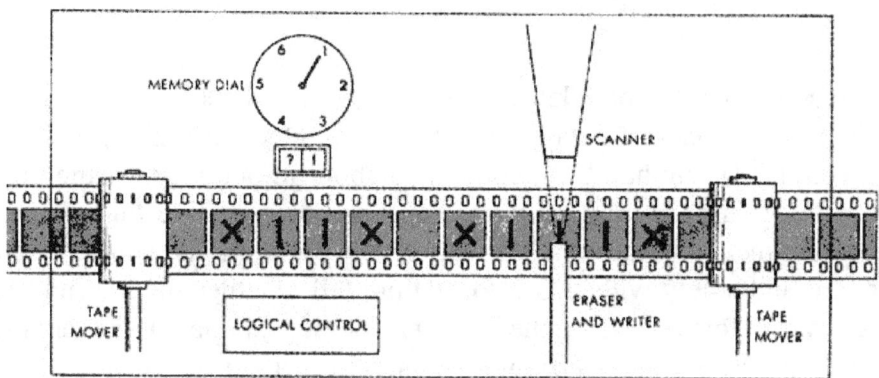

As you can see in the figure above, a Turing Machine consists of four parts: 1) An infinitely long *Tape* that is divided into cells. Each cell can hold symbols from a finite alphabet. The alphabet contains a special character called a *blank* 2) A read/write head that can read the contents of the cell and write into it. The tape is capable of moving in both directions and the movement occurs not continuously, but in discrete time corresponding to the ticks of a clock, 3) An *Action Table* that contains *instructions* executed by the machine. These instructions depend on the current *state* of the machine, i.e., the set of symbols on the tape at the current point of time as well as a set of instructions. The instructions can include the symbol to be written on the current square next to the head, and also the direction, left or right, to move the tape. 4) A *State register*, another table that contains all the states experienced by the Turing machine in its operations including the start state. Before the TM starts, a finite string of characters from the alphabet tape is written on the tape. This is the input string. The TM starts with the read/write head reading the first character of the input string. It then consults the action table and performs the action specified therein for that input character and the current state of the machine. It continues this process, moving the tape left or right, or writing characters onto the current square. Proceeding in this manner, a TM can either stop at some point, or run forever.

Turing also suggested an important extension of his TM, in which the action table of a TM is encoded as a string and then written into the input tape before a string describing the input. Such a TM is called a Universal Turing Machine because, as Turing showed, it could simulate any other TM. The UTM is an abstract model of modern computers because the program it executes can be read in as input rather than being 'hard-coded' in the action table of an ordinary TM.

Significance of the Turing Machine

In earlier chapters we have seen that humans have been trying to devise some form of computing machine for hundreds of years. Stonehenge, the Abacus, Charles Babbage's differential and analytical engines, were mechanical devices. The modern digital computer is based on electromagnetics and in just a few decades there have been numerous variations of these. The significance of the Turing Machine, is that, independent of the physical construction of a computer, it describes the underlying nature and operation of all of these in mathematical concepts and notation. Going even further, the *Church-Turing thesis* states that any computational procedure that is guaranteed to halt, i.e., any *algorithm*, can be simulated by a Turing machine. (Alonzo Church was a mathematician contemporary to Turing)

The Turing Machine enabled people to start thinking about theories of computation and researching important questions relating to computing. One particular problem that mathematicians predating Turing had been concerned about in one form or the other is called the *Halting Problem* and, in modern terms can be expressed like this: Can you write a computer program that can read *any* other computer program, as well as an input to that second program, and solely with this information, tell whether the second program will stop executing, or run forever. Using the Turing machine and related mathematics it is possible to give an answer: No, such a program cannot be written.

Impact on Future Technologies

The Turing Machine has profoundly impacted the way people think about computing and computers. The UTM inspired the design of modern computers in which a program is stored by the computer, read into memory, and then executed with a set of inputs (the set could be empty).

One result that came out of the TM is that to date no one has been able to come up with any kind of computing that cannot (theoretically) be performed by a Turing Machine. It has been conjectured with great confidence that no one will ever be able to do so. The Turing Machine also led directly to the birth of computing as a science and gave rise to the entire theory of computing, focused on understanding and predicting the behavior of algorithms and programs. In this way, the Turing Machine will have an impact on the future of computing for many years to come.

Concept Reinforcement:

1. What does the tape of a Turing Machine correspond to in a modern computer?

2. Why did the Turing Machine have such a great impact on the science of computing?

3. How does the Action Table of the Turing Machine cause a difference in the state of the machine?

Section 1.9 – The ENIAC

Section Objective:

- Understand the significance of the ENIAC on the science of computing, and analyze its impact on future technologies

What was the ENIAC?

The Electrical Numerical Integrator and Computer (ENIAC) was a computer developed in the years 1943 to 1946. It is regarded as the first general purpose programmable digital computer.

Origins

In the second world war, the Artillery units of the US army had a great need to develop firing tables. These are tables of data that enable those firing projectiles from cannons to choose firing angles taking into account the shape of the projectile, the wind conditions, distance to be reached and so on. Such tables are complex and tedious to calculate by hand and in 1943 the US army funded the Moore School of Engineering at the University of Pennsylvania to develop an automated means of computing firing tables. The project was headed by John Mauchly and J Presper Eckert.

An isolated valve tube.

Details

The ENIAC was 80 feet long, 8 feet tall and 3.5 feet wide. It was assembled by hand using nearly 17,500 valve (radio) tubes, and thousands each of other components like diodes, resistors, and capacitors. It could perform 5000 addition/subtractions and about 360 10 digit by 10 digit multiplications per second. Data could be input into the machine using an IBM punched card reader and an IBM card puncher could be used for hardcopy output.

The arithmetic operations were performed by 20 electronic components called accumulators, each capable of storing numbers up to 10 digits long. While addition could use all of these, multiplication, division and square root operations used subsets of the accumulators. Other components of ENIAC included a multiplier unit, an initiator for starting up the machine, a cycling unit used for synchronizing the operations of all the other components, a Master Programmer unit and others.

A picture of ENIAC.

The valve tubes generated lots of heat and were also unreliable, with several failing every day. It turned out that failures occurred just after the machine was started from a cold state, so, after 1948 the machine was never turned off and remained continuously on until 1955.

Significance

The ENIAC implemented a number of important techniques that became the cornerstones of modern computing. It used digital electronics, although based on valve tube technology, as opposed to the solid-state semiconductor electronics that was being developed at Bell Labs. ENIAC supported programming constructs like looping and 'if-then- else branching of program execution. Even though it had to be 'programmed' by the tedious process of reconnecting cables and flipping switches many regard it as the first general purpose electronic digital computer. In this context, general-purpose means that it was not designed to solve a specific type of mathematical problem but could do whatever the program told it to do. This was a leap over previous electronic computers such as the Colossus, built by the British army in 1942 whose hardware design was such that it could do only logical operations and no arithmetic.

It was able to do additions at least 100 times faster than the mechanical computers then in use. Thus, it showed once and for all that digital electronics was the future of computer science and engineering.

The ENIAC was 'programmed' by a team of women who physically moved cables and threw switches to change the computations performed by ENIAC. This could take up to two days, and to overcome this barrier, John von Neumann, a leading mathematician, with input from the ENIAC team suggested what has come to be known as the stored program architecture, also known as the von Neumann architecture. Here, the program instructions are treated as special input data that can be read into computer main memory and then executed on the 'real' data. By this means, the kinds of computations executed by the machine are not limited or controlled by its internal hardware and wiring. This idea effectively ended the notion that computers should be programmed by making hardware changes.

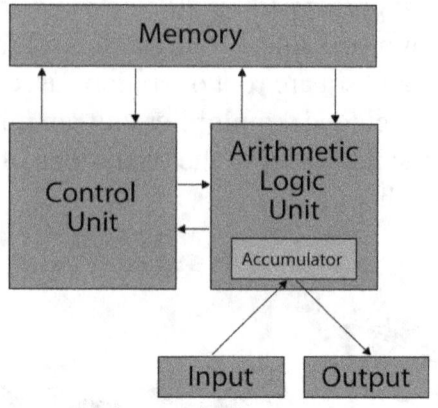

An example of von Neumann architecture.

Impact on Future Technologies

Possibly most important ENIAC inspired the transition into the von Neumann stored program architecture that all computers now follow. While ENIAC was modified to implement a first version of the von Neumann architecture, the EDVAC and the Manchester Mark I (University of Manchester, England) are regarded as the pioneer von Neumann machines. The fact that it was a general function computer, albeit with a tedious programming system, opened up computing for scientists and researchers of all kinds, not just those interested in creating firing tables or similar specialized applications. As the machine that sparked the design of the stored program architecture it has had enormous impact since all the mainstream computers used today have this architecture.

Mauchly and Eckert commercialized their work into a company that eventually became the giant UNIVAC Corporation.

Concept Reinforcement:

1. Explain how ENIAC can be regarded as a general purpose computer. What are the limitations to this point of view?

2. Why is the stored program architecture seen as a great advance over earlier methods of programming computers?

Section 1.10 – The Microprocessor

Section Objective:

- Understand the significance the microprocessor had on the science of computing, and analyze its impact on future technologies

What is a Microprocessor?

The 'heart' of any computer, which performs the arithmetic, the data manipulation, and applies a program to data, is the Central Processing Unit (CPU), also known simply as the processor. Processors contain several important components: the Arithmetic Logic Unit (ALU) does arithmetic and logical operations, a control unit that manages all its operations, and register(s) used to store data values and instructions.

Until the early to mid 1970s, CPUs tended to be very large in size consisting of several circuit boards interconnected by means of wiring. The boards contained numerous logic circuits arranged in intricate combinations to accomplish the desired operations. However, with the advent of the integrated circuit, it became possible to shrink all of these large components into a tiny rectangular chip not more than a square inch or two in area. The integrated chip is typically encased in a special material with the requisite input/output connections protruding outside, ready to be attached onto a circuit board containing connections to the keyboard, monitor, disk storage and so on.

A picture of two microprocessors.

Credit for inventing and patenting the first microprocessors, in the years 1971 – 1973, is usually attributed to both Texas Instruments and Intel. In the three decades since, the processing capacity, speed, and features of microprocessors have become vastly enhanced. The major American designers and manufacturers of microprocessors in the USA are large companies like Intel, Motorola, Texas Instruments, and AMD. To distinguish their technology from each other microprocessors are given model names like, Intel 4004, TMS 1000, Motorola 6805, Pentium, Itanium and a host of others.

Computer scientists and engineers compare microprocessors on the basis of numerous important attributes. These can interact in complex ways with each other to affect the performance of the processor.

One of these is the instruction width of the microprocessor. Roughly speaking, this is the maximum number of bits that a microprocessor can handle at any one time. In particular, this is related to the width of the registers on the microprocessor. The earliest microprocessors used 8-bit instructions at a time. Clearly, increasing the width can increase the processing capacity of the microprocessor enabling it to process more complex instructions as well as larger chunks of data, simultaneously. Most personal computers today have 16-bit processors or 32-bit ones. High-end computers have 64-bit processors.

Another attribute of microprocessors is their clock speed. As you may know, computers don't operate in continuous time. Instead, there is a crystal-based timing device, called a clock, which sends out a signal at regular discrete intervals. Data movement throughout the computer occurs only when the signal is sent out. In particular, the processor executes instructions and performs computations when it receives this clock signal. The clock speed that a processor can handle is one measure of its performance. A 1-Giga Hertz microprocessor can handle 1 billion clock signals per second and can therefore execute, at least theoretically, up to 1 billion data processing operations per second. Movement of data, and processing of instructions is, of course, equivalent to the movement of electronics through the microprocessor. This generates heat inside the microprocessor. Since excessive heat buildup can literally melt the processor, an upper limit is usually placed on the clock speed it can be subjected to. Computer scientists/engineers design heat dissipation technologies to increase the speed rating of microprocessors, with some designs utilizing water-based cooling systems.

There are many other important attributes of microprocessors. One that deserves mention is the number of transistors that can be placed inside it. The reason this is important is that logic gates consist of interconnected transistors. Thus, the number of transistors that can be packed into a microprocessor, or generally speaking, an integrated circuit, is a measure of its complexity and power.

Programming the Microprocessor

The software program instructions 'understood' by a microprocessor bear little similarity to the English-like computer languages (Visual BASIC, JAVA, C-Sharp) that most of us use. Instead, a microprocessor needs to have this program code converted into a special language often called Assembler language. There is no one Assembler language. Instead, each family of microprocessors from a particular manufacturer understands its own assembler language. A very famous such language is the Intel 8080 Assembler language that was designed for Intel's very successful 8080 family of microprocessors used in the original IBM PCs.

The microprocessor has had a very profound significance on computing. It led directly to the invention of the personal computer which, of course, made the power of complex information processing, databases, graphics, animation and a host of others, available to people worldwide. This in turn, has motivated the need for networking, data communications, and the explosion of the world-wide web.

It is important to note that the microprocessor is not confined to computers alone. The microprocessor is the basis for a whole host of electronic devices from printers, to graphics cards, to data communications equipment, to cell phones and others too numerous to mention. Modern automobiles and airplanes are equipped with sophisticated microprocessors that control many crucial functions.

On a more theoretical level, since microprocessors can be produced cheaply and in large quantities, they motivated the development of parallel and distributed computing. In both of these, a large array of microprocessors is combined to create a system that is more powerful than the sum of its parts. In fact, most modern super-computers consist of interconnected microprocessors together with sophisticated techniques to break down complex and large problems (such as weather prediction or playing chess well enough to beat a grandmaster) into smaller sub-problems that can be handled almost simultaneously by each of the hundreds of microprocessors in the system.

Impact on Future Technologies

The microprocessor is here to stay and to have an even more significant impact on computing for the foreseeable future. One reason for this is a prediction by Gordon Moore, a scientist and one of the founders of Intel, called Moore's law, which says, in essence, that every 18 months the number of transistors than can be packed economically into an integrated chip doubles. The consequences of such rapid increases in the processing power of microprocessors will be to enable the development of very powerful cell phones, make robots more functional and versatile, and other wonders that are difficult to even imagine today!

Concept Reinforcement:

1. What was the role of the integrated circuit in the development of the microprocessor?

2. What are some consequences of Moore's Law on microprocessors?

3. Explain how heat build-up can affect the performance of a microprocessor.

Section 1.11 – Past Programming Languages

Section Objective:

- Understand the significance past programming languages had on the science of computing, and analyze their impact on future technologies

What is a Programming Language?

A computer program is simply a set of instructions telling the computer what to do. As we have seen in an earlier chapter, the processor (CPU) of a computer receives instructions and data in a stream of binary words called machine language. However, humans find it really difficult to write complex series of instructions in terms of 0s and 1s. Programming Languages (PLs) were devised to look more like English and thereby make it easy to write complex programs, or, in other words, to do software development. Some examples of PLs are FORTRAN, ALGOL, BASIC, C, JAVA and many others. Writing a program is referred to as programming or coding and the resultant lines produced are called source code or just code.

Conversion to machine language

Of course the CPU still understands only machine language. So how is a program written with English-like words 'understood' by the CPU? This is accomplished by special programs called Compilers and Interpreters that take as input a program (or a line of a program) written in a PL containing English-like words and convert it into the 0s and 1s understood by the CPU. Compilers take a complete program consisting of tens or hundreds or thousands of lines of code and convert them into the machine language. The resulting strings of 0s and 1s is called compiled code, or just the binary. The programmer has to wait for the compiling process to be completed and only then use the resulting program, i.e., execute or run it.

Interpreters are more interactive: they accept one line of code at a time, compile and execute them, thus giving instant response. FORTRAN was always a compiled language. Early implementations of BASIC for personal computers like the APPLE II microcomputer were interpreted languages. However, to keep things simple, in this chapter we shall speak only of compilers.

Note that there is no single compiler. Instead for every pair consisting of a programming language and a specific family of processors a compiler must be written. Hence we speak of a C compiler for the 8088 family of processors rather than just a 'C compiler.'

Unlike the English language, which contains more than 300,000 words that can be used in almost countless combinations, PLs typically have a very limited vocabulary of say 50 or 60 words. These words provide functionality like reading from disk storage, writing back to storage, printing, and so on. PLs describe data input into the program using symbols called Variables. The power of using variables is that they refer not to a specific value (like 3, 4, 7.99) but to anyone of these at a given time depending on the input data and what the program does to them. This is, of course, one of the main strengths of computers. Instead of having to write new code to calculate the circumference of a circle every time for a different value of radius, the PL allows you to name an abstract variable as, say, the letter R and then encode a formula like:

C = 2 * PI* R. (Here PI stands for π).

This encoded formula can be used over and over again simply by giving as input a desired value of R.

A computer starts at the first line of a program and executes lines in succession until told by the program to skip to another one. When the computer is executing a particular line of a program we say that program control is at that line.

PLs also include the usual mathematical symbols like + and * (multiplication); these are known as operators. In addition, they have special sequences of words, called constructs, to perform certain special processes. One, called iteration, simply means repeating a set of instructions until told to stop. Here is an example:

N = 0

While (N < 20)

C = 2 * PI * N

Print C

N = N + 1

End While

This program fragment executes the statements between the While and End While 20 times.

A related construct is called Branching. One way of coding is by means of If…Then.. Else…End If statements. Example:

If Gender = 'M' then

Count_Males = Count_Males + 1

Else

Count_Females = Count_Females + 1

End if

This 'program' assumes that Gender can only be one of two values 'M' or 'F.' It can be used for counting the number of females and males in, say, a student roster. Note that the program executes a different line (goes down a different path) depending on the value of the variable Gender that it encounters.

Programming languages at the dawn of the computing era

Until the mid 1970s, computers were mostly used by scientists and engineers to perform complicated mathematical number crunching and calculation. They were seldom used for word processing, graphics, music and all the functionality we take for granted today. Therefore the early programming languages were chiefly designed to support scientific computing. One example of this is FORTRAN, short for Formula Translator. There were several versions of FORTRAN, going all the way to FORTRAN IV. One characteristic of FORTRAN is that lines of the program could be given numbers. Then, branching was accomplished by means of a statement like GO TO 2341. If the program encountered this GO TO statement control went to line 2341 and started executing all the following lines until the program either ended or another GO TO statement was encountered.

Other early computer languages were ALGOL, COBOL and several others.

Significance

The mere fact that computers could be programmed in English-like languages vastly increased the power of computing and the applications thereof. The early microcomputers were 'programmed' by pushing switches on a front panel and reading results of a row of lights. Even the early very expensive and large so-called mainframe computers like EDVAC were programmed by physically adding and removing connecting wires. Freed of this limitation, people did things with software that even the original creators of the programming language used could not have dreamed of.

Impact on Future Technologies

As they explored the limits and experienced the frustration of these early languages people learned more about the nature of software development and computers in general and developed better languages, more sophisticated constructs and learned to handle non-numeric data. This led to the kind of languages and computing capabilities we have today. Typically,computer and operating system vendors provide *software development kits* specially matched to the functionalities and capabilities of their products. Using these, programmers can create software that fully exploits the capabilities of the devices.

Concept Reinforcement:

1. Explain why Programming Languages were devised.

2. Identify two major constructs typically supported by most PLs.

3. Can you think of three reasons why a language like English, or French, or Spanish (so-called *natural* languages) is unsuitable as a Programming language?

Section 1.12 – The Personal Computer

Section Objective:

Understand the significance personal computer had on the science of computing, and analyze its impact on future technologies

What is a Personal Computer

A personal computer (PC) is a computer designed for the personal use of individuals who, most often, are not professional programmers. It contains a CPU (sometimes more than one) with associated circuitry and disk storage contained in a system unit, one or more displays, a keyboard, and a mouse. It can be connected to peripheral devices like a printer or scanner, and can be networked. Desktop PCs have system units encased in small cubical cases and rectangular displays that are typically anywhere from 15 inches to 22 inches long across the diagonal. Laptop computers combine the system unit, display, mouse, and keyboard into a portable package the size of a large book weighing anywhere from 5 to 9 lbs. The new class of ultra-portable notebook computers is even smaller and lighter, yet is fully functional.

History

A picture of Steve Wozniak.

The first personal computer, containing all the components described above (system unit, keyboard, display, disk storage) was designed by Steve Wozniak under the name Apple II by Apple Computer Inc. headed by Steve Jobs, in 1977 in Cupertino, California, located at the western edge of Silicon valley, about 40 miles south of San Francisco. It utilized the 6502 microprocessor and excited people with its color display. The introduction of the first spreadsheet, VisiCalc for the Apple II extended its use beyond hobbyists and programmers to the general public. Competing personal computers at that time included the Radio Shack TRS-80.

The success of the Apple II and its successors attracted the attention of the largest computer company of that time, IBM. In 1981, IBM released its version of a personal computer, the IBM PC based on the Intel 8088 family of processors and utilizing an operating system called DOS from an obscure company called Microsoft. The IBM PC was also hugely successful and one of its consequences was the great success and growth of Microsoft.

The next big step in the evolution of Personal Computers was the revolutionary Macintosh, based on the Motorola 68000 microprocessor, from Apple Inc, in 1984. This machine introduced the mouse pointing device with access to any point on the screen, a graphical display, and other innovations both hardware and software. Until then most displays showed only discrete lines containing discrete characters and changing fonts required a huge effort.

The Macintosh borrowed most of these innovations from their inventor: Xerox's Palo Alto Research Center (PARC) located just west of Silicon Valley on Coyote Hill Road. The mouse was invented by an engineer called Douglas Engelbart when he was at another silicon valley company called SRI, located in Menlo Park.

A few years later Microsoft introduced its version of all these innovations under the name Windows. Today the vast majority of computers are based on the Windows operating system and still utilize CPUs based on the original 8086 family, albeit vastly improved. The macintosh holds its own, though, and Apple's line of laptop computers is also greatly prized.

The introduction of new models of PCs was greatly facilitated by rapid advances in the power of microprocessors, memory chips, disk storage, video cards and similar hardware by companies like Motorola, Texas Instruments, Intel and countless others.

One crucial difference between Apple's computers and the others is that Apple jealously guards both the hardware and the operating system, refusing to license either of these to third party manufacturers. On the other hand, Microsoft licenses its Windows operating system to hardware manufacturers. This has enabled a host of hardware designs, and third-party plug-in components, both hardware and software to be developed worldwide. Major manufacturers of Windows computers include HP, Dell, SONY, Toshiba and others.

Significance

Up to the late 1970s computers were big hulking assemblies of metal and wires and electronic components called mainframe computers. These occupied vast air-conditioned rooms with raised floors and were touchable only by a privileged priesthood. Users had to submit programs on punched cards and collect the output at the computer's convenience on paper print-outs. Interactivity was limited. The PC changed all that. Suddenly, the power of computing became available to everyone, from pre-teens to grand-parents. This led to a huge burst of creativity from hardware designers as well as software programmers to develop creative products and applications.

A young boy using a laptop.

The personal computer is one of the major technological innovations of mankind. Innovation has been rapid and the cost of these machines has also decreased dramatically. Future directions include miniaturization to cell phones and tablets of all sizes.

Concept Reinforcement:

1. Identify two advantages of personal computers over the earlier mainframe computers.

2. What do you think: will the cell phone someday replace a laptop computer?

Section 1.13 – Data Communications and Networking

Section Objective:

- Understand the significance of data communications and networking had on the science of computing, and analyze its impact on future technologies

What is Data communications?

Data communications is the science and technology that enables the interchange of information between computers. When multiple computers are interconnected by means of wires or wirelessly, and can communicate data among themselves, the computers are said to be networked. Clearly networking cannot occur without seamless and speedy data communications. In a future chapter we shall study networking. Here we focus on data communications.

Basics of Data Communications

As you have learned form earlier chapters, information processing within a computer occurs by the manipulation of binary electrical signals, i.e., signals that can be in only one of two voltage levels at any given time. Correspondingly, data communication also occurs by the transmission and receipt of binary signals. However, these binary signals are not necessarily in the form of two voltages when transmitted over a wire or wirelessly. Instead, a network interface card in the computer converts the binary voltages into another form, for example, changing the amplitude of a waveform. Each NIC has built into it a unique Media Access Control (MAC) address, typically a 48 bit or 64 bit number.

The rate at which these binary signals are sent out over a network is often referred to as the network speed. We can speak of these binary signals as 0s and 1s. Thus, a computer transmits a stream of 0s and 1s through its network card and other computers receive this stream via their network cards. To enable all these computers to understand these streams, so that a transmitting computer can be confident that others on the network get exactly what was sent out, is accomplished by establishing standards, or protocols. These protocols,called the ISO/OSI Basic Reference Model (or simple as the OSI Model) were established by the International Standards Organization. OSI stands for Open Systems Interconnect. A protocol specifies one or both of the formats of data streams as well as methods for processing the data stream. However, the protocols are not actual software or hardware. It is left up to manufacturers such as CISCO to develop the hardware and software as they please so long as they follow the protocols.

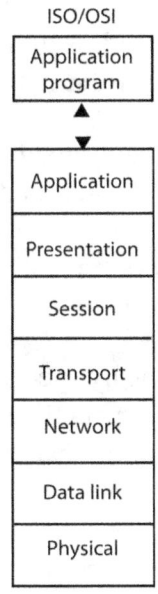

ISO/OSI

Application program

Application
Presentation
Session
Transport
Network
Data link
Physical

ISO/OSI model.

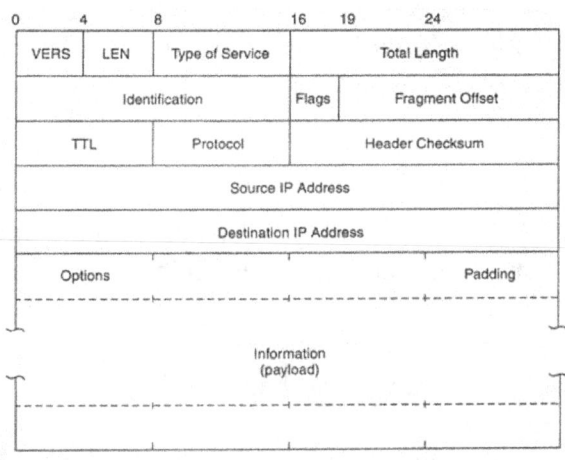

A picture of a typical IP packet.

Data transmission protocols

It was somewhat natural that in the 1950s and 1960s when data communications and net-working were first being researched, the starting point would be the telephone system. In a telephone system, even when someone is calling long distance, like San Francisco from Boston, the telephone system essentially dedicates a physical wire to the conversation. It probably consists of many pieces, but once the connection is made, this wire remains until the parties hang up. This technology is called circuit switching.

In data communications, however, a long data stream (sequence of 1s and 0s) is broken up at its origin into smaller pieces called packets.

A system that is popular for wired data communications within a building or small network (a Local Area Network, LAN) is called Ethernet. Before sending out a packet (containing the MAC address of a destination computer) this protocol first checks whether the outgoing cable is free of other signals. If so, it sends out the packet. If not it waits a random number of milliseconds and then tries again. Note that electrical signals travel very fast over wires (sometimes as much as one tenth the speed of light), so success is usually guaranteed unless there are too many computers on the Ethernet.

To get a packet to the destination computer outside of a local area network requires use of the IP protocol. Here, each packet has a header and a trailer in a specified format depending on the protocol and also a sequence number. The header contains the IP address of the destination computer. This address is typically four bytes separated by periods, like 192.13.178.101.

The physical movement of packets is done by specialized devices like routers, hubs, switches and others. Such devices are actually specialized computers, with processors, memory and data interfaces. They read each incoming packet and specifically the destination IP address. Then the router consults a routing table. This is a database of destination IP addresses and possible in-between routers' addresses. The router selects one of these and sends the entire packet onwards. After a series of hops the packet finally arrives at its destination. This technology is called packet switching.

Note that a long stream of data from the source could be broken into many packets and each packet could take a different route. Assembling all of these in an error-free way is the function of the TCP protocol (Transmission Control Protocol).

Physical medium

The lowest level of the ISO/OSI standards is concerned with the physical medium used for data communications. A variety of media are used. Telephone wires were used in the early days but nowadays CAT-5 cables, fiber optics and wireless methods are the norm. Fiber optics uses glass fibers that use light waves of varying frequency to large number of data streams simultaneously, i.e., they have high bandwidth. Photo-electronic devices convert electrical signals into optical signals before transmission and vice versa on exit from the glass fiber. These are typically used for long distances such as within and between cities. The main data highways between the USA and Europe consist of undersea fiber. These have been rated at 2. 56 Trillion (10^{12}) bits/second.

Wireless networks have limited range such as the floor of a building, but newer technologies could extend that range considerably.

Significance

Putting it simply, the need for data communications has had great impact on computer science and technology. It enabled enormous advances in parallel and distributed computing so that supercomputer can be built from a collection of off-the-shelf low cost and relatively less powerful components including micro-processors. Of course data communications is the enabling technology for the world wide web.

Data communications will continue to be an active area of research and development. Nowadays, a file size of 50 Mbyte is considered rather large and cannot be sent via email. However, music, videos and entire movies are in the order of gigabytes. Video conferencing, voice over the web, web cams, and similar require very large amounts of data to be sent in real-time even across continents. Therefore, data communications technologies are constantly being improved to handle these kinds of demands.

Concept Reinforcement:

1. Explain the difference between circuit switching and packet switching.

2. Why is it that different packets in the same message could take different physical routes to the destination?

Section 1.14 – The World Wide Web

Section Objective:

- Understand the significance of the world wide web on the science of computing, and analyze its impact on future technologies

What is the world wide web?

Everyone has used the world wide web (www). It is a network of interconnected computers each of which runs software called a web server. Other interconnected computers use web client software like web browsers to gain access to a particular web server and read or write documents at that computer. These documents are in a special format called hyper text markup language (HTML) that enable links to other http documents and also to multimedia format documents such as audio, images, video, as well as databases.

Every web server (web site) receives a unique name called a Uniform Resource Locator (URL) that looks something like http://www.whitehouse.gov/infocus/education/. The first part of this, between the www and the / is also known as a domain name. Examples are www.amazon.com, www.uth.tmc.edu and so on. Examples of web server software are Microsoft's IIS (Internet Information Server) and the public domain Apache web server. Examples of web browsers are Microsoft Explorer, Mozilla Firefox, Opera and others.

Brief History

During the 1980s computer networking steadily increased in sophistication to the point that data could reliably be exchanged, broadcasted and programs executed on remote computers via the Internet. Examples of internet software included email, news groups, ftp (file transfer protocol) In 1991, Tim Berners-Lee a British computer scientist working at CERN, the European centre for nuclear research, in Geneva, Switzerland (actually at the Swiss-French border) developed the world wide web. In just a few years, the web became the dominant method of accessing information over the Internet.

Some details

An important feature of the special document format called HTML, in which web pages are customarily written, is the notion of a hyperlink, i.e., a line within the document that when clicked upon takes the user to other documents. Another important feature of HTML is (in the first few years at least) its simplicity. Unlike Microsoft word documents that are saved in complicated formats accessible only by itself, HTML documents are basically text in which the display qualities of each element are set by a simple markup language. This simplicity means programs that could read these web pages from remote locations could easily be developed. Such programs are called web browsers, which have rapidly advanced to the present level of sophistication that we now take for granted.

Although we access web servers by means of English-like names, the URLs in each web server has a numeric identifier called its IP address. The form of an IP address is A.B.C.D where each A, B, C, D is a whole number between 1 and 255, eg, 192.33.124.132. When you go to a web registry like that maintained by the domain registry company called Network Solutions, you receive the exclusive rights to that domain name. After you tell Network Solutions the IP address of your web server, the mapping between the name you reserved, and the numerical IP address is published into a database kept on Domain Name Servers. There are numerous DNS's on the internet that constantly update each other's domain name databases.

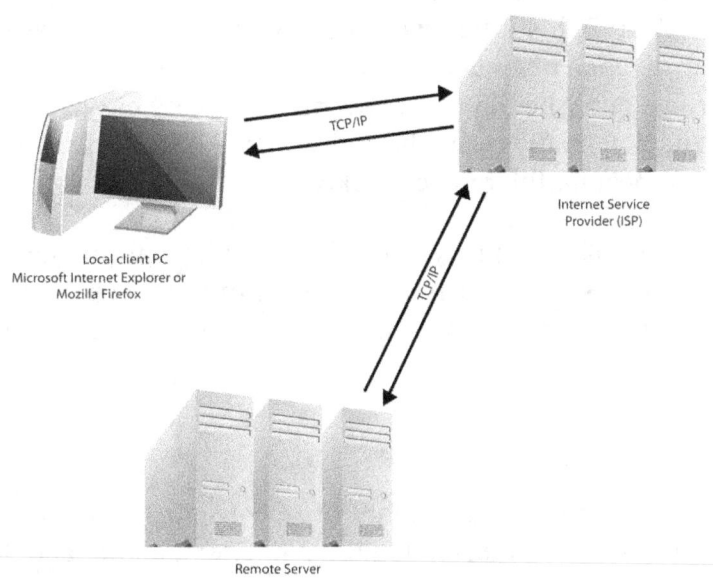

How it works (very briefly)

Underlying the world wide web is the hypertext transfer protocol (http). This is a prescribed standard, agreed upon worldwide, by which messages consisting of binary digits are formatted and sent across the internet. In addition, http specifies the actions that must be taken by web browsers and servers in response to specific http commands. For example, when you go to a browser running on your computer, and type in the command http://www.disney.com, and hit enter, the browser converts the entire string into 0s and 1s according to the http format. This is sent from your computer to the internet by a collection of computing hardware, the name www.disney.com is resolved to its IP address by a domain name server and thence to the physical computer that runs the domain www.disney.com. The web server here then looks for a special starting HTML format document pointed to by the web server as the home page, and passes these bytes back to the web browser on your computer. The web browser reads this html document from top to bottom, interprets each HTML markup command and displays it on your computer.

Of course, there are numerous details and technologies that must work in order to make all this happen. Considerable, and remarkably rapid, progress was made in the science and technology of fiber optics. Special equipment called routers, hubs, and switches enable the web as we know it. Software engineers devised innovative algorithms to create all kinds of amazing applications running on the web. Chat, instant messaging, web-based email are but a few of these. In addition, there are systems like web-ex that enable video conferencing between people in Beijing, San Francisco, London, and Sydney (Australia) to talk and see each other in real time. People in these far-flung locations can even collaboratively work on the same document together in near-real time.

Significance

In just a few years, from the early 1990s to the present day, the web has become amazingly sophisticated and indispensable. It touches on almost every activity that we do. Because technologies have been devised to enable almost anyone, without any specialized training in computing, to create a sophisticated web site at very low cost, it has enabled what may be called the democratization of content. Whereas it takes a lot of effort and money to print a book or get an article published in a print journal, it is very easy and cheap to broadcast one's information and potentially reach the entire world. (Of course, this doesn't mean the content is accurate or meaningful, or even makes sense!)

From an economic point of view the web has led to entire information industries becoming more and more web-based. Advertising, purchase of consumer products, buying entire vacations, and almost everything else that we do add up to transactions worth multiple billions of dollars daily.

Impact on Future Technologies

The web will continue to spark the creativity of scientists and engineers to develop even more innovative applications and technologies. While text, audio, and video are the principal forms of media served up on the web, scientists have worked on transmitting other information such as aromas and textures. Of course these require special hardware at the client side. Internet-based telephony threatens conventional phone systems and very high quality complete movies on demand are not too far away. The role of the web in modern life, industry and commerce will become even more ubiquitous as cell phones and mobile devices get even more integrated with the web.

Concept Reinforcement:

1. What is the difference between the Internet and the World wide web?

2. What functionality does a DNS provide?

3. What is the role of HTTP in the world wide web?

Section 1.15 – Web Servers and Clients: Significance in the Science of Computing

Section Objective:

- Understand the significance of web servers and clients on the science of computing, and analyze its impact on future technologies

What are Web servers and clients?

A web client is software that enables computers to communicate with and get information from web sites. The overwhelming majority of web clients in common user today are web browsers like Internet Explorer, Firefox, Netscape, and Opera.

In the most general sense, a web server consists of the computers and the software that presents web pages comprising its web site to web browsers.

A web page is a text file written in the format and syntax specified by the hypertext markup language (HTML), and containing formatted text, pictures, videos and links to other web pages within that particular web site and to other locations. The name of the web site, also called its Uniform Resource Locator (URL), confirms to the conventions of the HyperText Transfer Protocol (HTTP), a standard method by which information is transferred from the web server to a web browser. Note that the name of a web site is an alphabetical version of its IP address. The IP address consists of four numbers, each between 1 and 255 connected by periods. These add up to 32 bits.

Web server Hardware

The hardware portion of a web server consists of one or many interconnected computers, and also the various networking hardware such as routers, switches, hubs, firewalls, fiber optic cables, CAT5 cables enabling data communications. The operating systems of these computers are typically Microsoft Windows, or LINUX, or UNIX. The entire system can be either monolithic, or consist of just a few powerful systems, or be composed of a cluster of many hundreds of smaller boxes. In addition, the hardware could also include powerful database servers that are computers connected to large banks of databases on magnetic media and running database management software like Microsoft's SqlServer, ORACLE, or the open source MySQL. There may also be specialized database servers optimized to provide data-intensive content such as images, music, and video.

Large corporations like Microsoft locate their web site hardware in locations that they own. For redundancy and for enhancing access speeds, they may locate their web sites in multiple locations across the USA. They may also choose to have physical locations in the countries they operate in. Smaller companies may not even own their own hardware. Instead they install their web site content web pages in co-location sites where hundreds of companies share hardware.

Web server software is the software running on the web server hardware that responds to requests from web browsers. For convenience we shall call this simply server software. Two commonly used server software packages are Microsoft's Internet Information Server (IIS), and the open-source Apache.

When users, via a web browser, type in the name of a web site (i.e., its URL), this is treated as an http request. Then via the internet Domain Name server, it is sent to the web site of that name.

Web site Architecture

In theory, it is possible to run an entire web site off a Windows laptop using just internet server software (like IIS) and a locally running database server. The web pages comprising your web site could make requests to the database using a language called Active Server Pages (ASP) that is similar to Visual Basic. ASP allows you to put interesting controls like drop-downs on your web page, and also to create web-based forms. In addition, ASP can be used to connect to the database via technologies called ADO (Active Data Object) and ODBC (Open Database Connectivity).

Note that ASP scripts are located within the HTML pages comprising your web site. It is the job of the server software to handle all the requests generated within the web pages, and serve the results back to the client browser.

This simple 2-tier (synonymous with layer) system is too limited and cannot provide the rich interactivity, speed and other capabilities demanded of modern web sites. Instead, most professional web sites use a four (or more) tier logical architecture, as seen in the figure below.

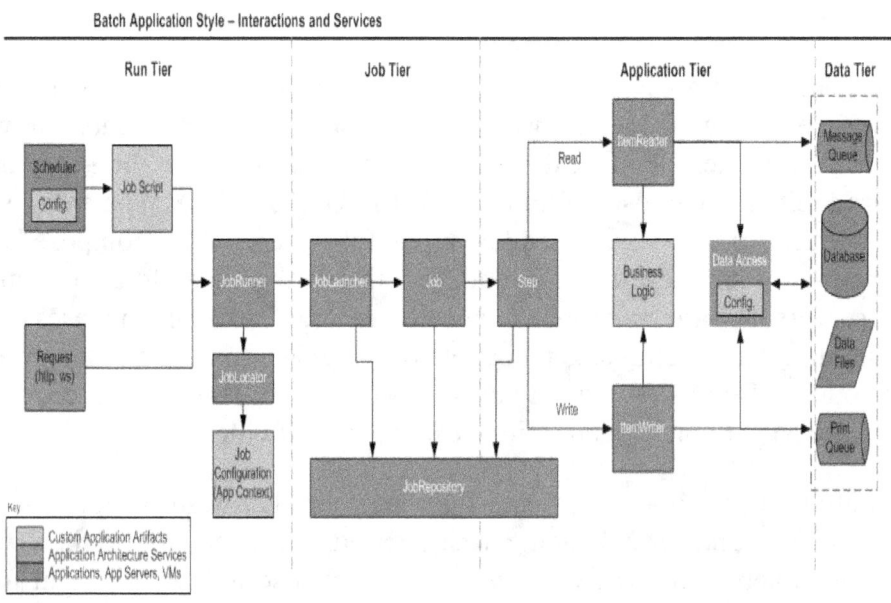

Here, the first tier consists of the web pages, written in HTML. These web pages contain ASP scripts comprising the second tier. The third tier consists of a collection of executable programs that were typically written in a higher level language like Visual C++ or Visual Basic and then compiled. For this reason, the third tier is sometimes called the COM tier. Because these programs are compiled, they can execute at high speed and because they are written in high-level languages, they can handle a much greater variety of data processing requests and provide a rich collection of features and behaviors. The last tier consists of the database management system and the associated data.

The flow of information is that a user first accesses the web pages and then clicks on the user interface of an ASP script. This gets sent to the 3rd tier and the compiled programs handle the request. If the request needs access to the database, the COM tier packages the request in the language of the Database Management System and sends the request to the 4th tier. The DBMS gets the data, or makes updates, and returns the response to the COM layer. The programs here then send the information back to the ASP layer which presents the information back to the first tier, redrawing the pages if needed.

It is important to note that the multi-layer architecture described above is a logical architecture. By this we mean that there is no requirement dictated by the architecture that each of the separate components should physically execute on different sets of machines. In practice, of course, the components of the logical architecture are distributed across multiple hardware.

Significance

Web servers and clients have been the enabling technologies for the powerful medium known as the world wide web that, in less than 15 years has permanently changed the way humans work, teach, learn, and live. These technologies have been the foundation of trillion dollar industries. Computer scientists and engineers have had to invent new technologies and perform innovative research and development to make this phenomenon happen.

Impact on Future Technologies

The web continues to grow and expand, and provide information in multiple ways. Web access from mobile small format devices like PDAs and cell phones requires clever modifications of web browsers and servers. As the demand for web access to rich media content grows, there will be a corresponding need for better web servers and browsers. These technologies will continue to grow and innovate.

Concept Reinforcement:

1. Why is a 2-tier architecture insufficient for running complex and rich web sites?

2. What is the role of the Database Management System in the 4-tier web site architecture?

3. What is the role of the ASP tier in a 4 tier web site architecture.

Unit Two

Section 2.1 – Algorithms

Section Objective:

- Understand the significance that algorithms have on the science of computing, and analyze their impact on future technologies

What is an Algorithm?

An algorithm is a step-by-step procedure that is guaranteed to terminate. It is a sequence of instructions to perform a task. For example, cook-books are full of recipes that describe how to make various dishes. Note that all recipes give you instructions on when to stop. For example "Bake at 400 degrees for 30 minutes, or until a toothpick inserted in the center comes out clean." These are examples of stopping rules.

Here we are concerned with algorithms to perform computational tasks. These include calculating mathematical formulas like that for the conversion of Celsius to Fahrenheit, adding up 300 consecutive numbers starting from 1, finding the area of a circle, determining body mass index and so on. For these problems, computational formulas exist. For example, the formula for the area of a circle is πr^2. The algorithm for computing the area of a circle can be written as:

Get the value of the radius, r.

Perform the multiplication π times r times r.

Print out the result

Stop.

However, there are many other computational tasks for which a formula does not exist. Arranging a set of numbers (or words) in ascending (alphabetical) order, searching a document for a given word, and similar. For these, the algorithms can be more complicated. An algorithm for sorting a list of numbers is the following.

- Start: Count the size of the list. Denote by N.

- Compare the first element of the list of N elements against all the others and discover the smallest. Set it aside in the first location in a *destination list*.

- (Note that there are now N-1 numbers in the remaining unsorted list)

- Now repeat step number 2 for the *remaining* unsorted list until the remaining list is empty. At each execution of step 2, the smallest number found is assigned a place *after* the existing ones in the destination list.

- Stopping rule: Terminate the algorithm when the remaining list is empty

This algorithm is known as the Bubble-sort algorithm. It may interest you to know that there is more than one algorithm for sorting a set of numbers (or words).

Significance

Algorithms underlie almost anything and everything in computer science. The function of a computer program is to implement one or more algorithms. In this sense, we say that programs *encode* algorithms. Without the notion of algorithms, and the mathematical study of algorithms, none of the benefits and vast functionality of computing that we use daily would exist.

The founders of Google courtesy of Joe Ito.

Devising a clever algorithm for some computational task can lead to great rewards. The founders of Google, Inc, who are very financially successful, invented the Page-Rank algorithm that streamlines searching the World Wide Web by assigning each page a rank. The basic idea (the algorithm used in practice is *much* more complex) is this: to assign a rank to a web page (lets call it P for convenience) look at the rank of each page that links to P, divide that by the number of outbound links coming out of it and add up these ratios. You may notice that this definition is circular: to calculate the rank of a page you need to know the ranks of the other pages. Such an algorithm is called a *recursive algorithm*, and can be made to terminate in various ways.

Impact on Future Technologies

Typically, computer science students take one or more courses devoted to understanding existing algorithms, techniques for analyzing how good they are, and systematic ways to develop new ones. Many students find this the most exciting (and challenging!) part of the computer science. As computers begin to tackle ever more complex tasks and challenges, developing good and effective algorithms to solve these problems will be even more important. It cannot be emphasized enough that algorithms underlie all of computing in one way or the other.

Concept Reinforcement:

1. Explain why the bubble-sort algorithm given above will always terminate, no matter how large the input list of numbers.

2. How can you extend the bubble-sort algorithm to sorting a list of 3 letter words?

3. A recipe in a cookbook gives detailed descriptions and quantities of ingredients. It ends by saying: "Mix well and bake at 415 degrees". Is this an algorithm? Explain why or why not.

Section 2.2 – Currently Used Programming Languages

Section Objective:

- Understand the significance of currently used programming languages on the science of computing, and analyze its impact on future technologies

Programming Languages of Today.

In an earlier chapter we learned what a programming language (PL) is and the names of a few that were popular during the 60s and 70s, when computing mostly concentrated on scientific and engineering problems.

To meet the rising expectations of people from computing, people started writing more and more complex programs and also started using computers for more than just science and engineering. Hence the newer languages like BASIC, PASCAL, PL-1 started providing more built-in support for manipulating not only numbers, but also letters, words, and more complex data structures that used other basic data types as building blocks. For example a person's name is a data structure that consists of three parts: first, middle, and last names, plus suffixes like 'Jr' and 'Sr'. Each of these is a string of characters and a data structure for a persons name could consist of 4 strings called FirstName, MidName, LastName, and Suffix.

It was soon realized that industrial-strength programming is a very complex activity and that writing long, correct, fully debugged programs (see the section 1-2-15) can be very difficult. Hence computer scientists began developing languages that could aid in this task. In addition, they developed a methodology called Object-oriented programming (OOP) in which specific data and the methods that are appropriate to operate on that data are combined into an entity called an object. For example, consider an object called 'RegularPolygon'. Of course there are many kinds of regular polygons, but they are all 2-dimensional figures, bounded by straight lines of equal length. They have names like square, pentagon, hexagon depending on the number of sides. Each type of regular polygon has a formula (methods) for its perimeter and surface area. The RegularPolygon object can include all these definitions and methods as lines of code.

An object-oriented program is based open collections of objects of varying complexity that are called upon when needed by the program logic. Examples of OOP languages are JAVA, Visual Basic, C++, C-Sharp. Among the many useful features supported by OOP are inheritance, overloading, information hiding, encapsulation, and reusability. However, descriptions of these are beyond the scope of this chapter.

Current programming languages also offer built-in support for error handling, and exception handling, i.e., situations when the program encounters unexpected events while running.

Another important development in programming is the Integrated Development Environment (IDE) that combines a program editor with the compiler, and tools for debugging. This has enormously enhanced programmer productivity.

Specialized and Fourth Generation languages.

While JAVA, C++ and similar are general purpose languages, in the sense that they can be used to write programs for all conceivable types of data and applications, some specialized PLs are also in use today, focused on specific applications and data. PERL focuses on manipulating strings and text. ASP, PHP, and Java Script, are used to help create sophisticated web sites. SQL and PL-SQL are used for database programming, and many others.

In addition, there are so-called Fourth Generation languages (4GLs) that were developed to perform complex operations in specialized areas. Many go beyond merely writing lines of code, to being complete systems with sophisticated user interfaces. For example, SAS and SPSS are 4GLs used to perform statistical data analysis. MATLAB and Mathematica are used for mathematical programming and scientific visualization. One of the latter's strengths is symbolic mathematics which means that it can not only perform numerical applications but can also do higher order mathematical operations such as algebra and calculus.

Significance

OOP provides many benefits to help teams of programmers develop large complex programs. One of these is that objects can be named and compiled into libraries (sometimes called Dynamic Linked Libraries, DLLs). Each object can be used by means of its API (Application Program Interface) which defines the way that other programs can utilize the object when needed. While the easy availability of sophisticated PLs and associated IDEs have greatly enhanced programmer productivity, it should be noted that poorly functioning programs can still be written even in spite of using these tools!

The need for better ways to write software and understand its behavior is never-ending. This has given rise to a branch of computer science called Formal Methods that applies advanced mathematics to model the fundamental logic flow of programs. Their research provides a formal basis for advanced programming constructs like multi-threading, concurrency control and similar. The former refers to multiple logic flows being executed by a single program and the latter is concerned with making sure these separate threads operate in a coordinated way.

Impact on Future Technologies

Every new generation of PLs pushes further the boundaries of what can be achieved by computing. Some interesting future application areas are cell phone programming, also known as app programming, and robotics.

Concept Reinforcement:

1. Assume that a particular PL allows data structures but has built-in support only for two data types: numerals (0,1,2,…9), and single characters (A, B, C,… Z,). Describe a data structure for entries in a phone book.

2. In addition to computing surface area, what other methods could be that of the Regular Polygons object described earlier? What are some operations would not be appropriate to include in this object?

Section 2.3 – Design

Section Objective:

- Understand the significance of design on the science of computing, and analyze its impact on future technologies

What is design?

Design has several meanings in the context of computing. One is the outward appearance of the device, also known as product design. While some manufacturers seem to merely throw components together, other computer companies obviously pay a lot of attention to making their products easy to use and aesthetically appealing. Software design can include its user interface (sometimes called the look and feel) as well as the allocation of functionality among program components and their inter-relationships. Hardware design is concerned with the selection and assembly of the various components of computing devices in order to meet desired performance, pricing, weight, power consumption, heat emission and similar goals.

Due to the rapid pace of advances in technology, system designers have to make sure their product is not behind the competition by the time it is tested, thoroughly debugged, and released. In addition, the design of computing devices is especially complex because software is often embedded in special purpose processors and can interact with the hardware to affect overall system performance. For example, a video card can have complex 3-D graphics software encoded into the processor. The hardware design has to be compatible with the software to ensure meeting design goals. Finally, another complication is that a typical computing component is often sourced from multiple organizations that could be scattered all over the world, or from different components of the same company.

To help systems designers accomplish their tasks scientists and engineers realized that it would be helpful if a set of industry standards could be devised that would be followed by all interested parties and serve as a common basis for design and development of software and hardware products. These are guidelines that spell out at least at high level, substantive details of the proposed product while leaving enough flexibility for engineers and scientists to innovate. For example, the IEEE 754-1985 standard for representing floating point numbers describes levels of precision based on the number of bits needed to store such numbers. A single precision floating point number is defined in this standard as 32 bits long with the sign of the number as the leftmost bit, the next 8 bits for the exponent, and the remainder for the fraction.

Real (Floating Point 32)																
Bit #	31	30	29	28	27	26	25	24	23	22	21	20	19	18	17	16
	Sign	Exponent								Mantissa						
Bit #	15	14	13	12	11	10	9	8	7	6	5	4	3	2	1	0
Mantissa																

A representation of 32-bit floating notation.

For electrical engineering and computer science the main organization that is responsible for creating standards is the Institute for Electrical and Electronics Engineers (IEEE, called I-triple-E). This is a prestigious international organization of scientists, engineers, physicist and mathematicians, all with interests in any form of electricity-based technology, with 365,000 members worldwide, headquartered in New York City. Its Standards Association (IEEE-SA) is the sub-organization devoted to making and establishing industry-wide standards in multiple fields. It is estimated that about 1000 standards have been established and a few hundred more are being developed. The IEEE also has about 35 societies, each for an aspect of electrical technology, such as the IEEE Computer Society, IEEE Communications society. These societies are typically the sponsors of standards in their particular focus. A proposed new IEEE standard must first gain approval from the IEEE-SA board. Next, a working group of scientists and engineers is selected to develop the standard. A balloting group of IEEE members who are interested in the subject matter is also created. Drafts of the standard are sent by the working group to the balloting group and if it gains approval from at least 75% of the latter, the draft is sent to the IEEE-SA.Review Committee.. After passing the RevCom the IEEE-SA board must still approve it.

Currently, a set of standards of interest to many are the IEEE 802.11 standards for Wireless Networks (WiFi). The first was released in 1997. Multiple standards, such as 802.11a, 802.11b, 802.11g, exist since the technology is constantly evolving and improving. Each standard specifies the wireless frequency to be used, the target data rates, the data transport technology and other details. For example, the 802.11n standard, to be released in 2009 specifies a data rate of 248Mbits per second. Manufacturers can read this standard and have a common basis for designing and developing compatible WiFi routers and adapters.

Significance

Innovative design and integration of multiple components have been keys to the success and adoption of computing and networking devices. Computer scientists and engineers have developed many innovations to provide functionality in response to product design demands. Miniaturization of hard drives and data storage in general was driven by the design goal of packing as many bytes as possible into ever smaller form factors. This led directly to the development of highly portable MP3 players.

Impact on Future Technologies

Without the standards process there would be multiple competing designs and products for the same computing technologies. A laptop with a built in WiFi adapter from some manufacturer would be unable to connect wirelessly to the internet unless the wireless router was also from the same manufacturer. Clearly, this would reduce portability and have adverse effects on the technology and its adoption. Thus, industry standards have contributed to the dissemination of computing technology.

The impact of design in future computing will become even more interesting as robotics and mobile computing/communications continue to innovate and develop.

Concept Reinforcement:

1. Explain how design goals can impact technology development.

2. What is the role of industry standards in computing technology?

3. Describe the impact of standards on future technologies.

Section 2.4 – Databases

Section Objective:

- Understand the significance of Databases on the science of computing, and analyze its impact on future technologies

What is a DataBase?

In the widest sense, any collection of data/information saved in permanent storage (like disk or tape) and accessible by a computer is a database. In practice the term database implies an organized and structured collection of data that is managed, accessed, created, and edited by means of a special kind of software called a Database Management System (DBMS). The physical storage medium can be magnetic disk, CDs, DVDs, or flash drives (thumb drives). Until recently, reel-to-reel tapes were also a popular medium of long term storage. These have been supplanted with disk-based formats because the latter tend to be faster to access, and can be more durable. In addition, tape-based storage is accessed sequentially, in the sense that to get a particular data item you have to spin the tape until that point is reached. On the other hand, disks support random access, i.e., you can go right to a desired data item on the disk without having to go through intervening locations. Thus, disks provide faster access. For these reasons, we shall speak only of disks as storage media.

A file is a named collection of data on a disk. You can create files using software like a word processor, or a spreadsheet or a painting program, or a music software. There are many types of information that can be created and stored on a computer. While this is changing, most DBMSs today focus on storing simple kinds of data such as text, and numbers. For example, the roster of students in your school, their grades, schedules and so on are kept in a database. (Possibly the database may also have student identity pictures).

Databases in computer science

The science of databases was an important topic of research in the late 1970s and 1980s. The issues that computer scientists had to face was how best to organize collections of data, even if located in a single file, so that it could be used to maximum benefit. One very important concern was to create an organization and structure to enable fast and easy Query. This refers to being able to access questions and have the database provide the answers speedily. For example with the student database a school administrator may want to ask queries like:

"What were Jack Smith's grades in Math in middle school?"

"How many students scored at least a B in Social Studies in the Fall 2008 semester in grade 9?"

Other tasks one may want to do is to add a new student, remove those who have passed out, create reports, rearrange data in alphabetical order and a host of others.

The data organization that became hugely popular, and remains so today, is called a Relational Database. In this organization, a collection of related data (students in a school, rooms in a building, books in a library) are organized into one or more two dimensional Tables. A table also consists of a set of data related in some way that share common attributes. For example, each student in a student database will have attributes like a social security number, first, middle, and last name, age, date of birth, address, name of father, name of mother, phone number, color of eyes, color of hair, and so on. The columns of the table comprise the attributes and the rows consist of individual students.

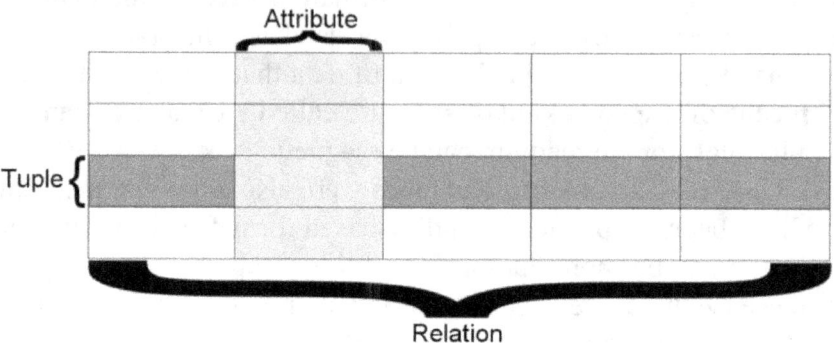

An example of a relational database.

A relational database can have multiple tables linked together by common data items called keys. When creating a database, there are several steps. The first, to understand all the separate data items, attributes, and their relationships to each other is called data modeling. Another important task includes the design of tables and identification of keys. There are numerous tasks in developing a database and these can involve database architects, database programmers, report writers and others. Database programmers are usually experts in writing queries. The most common language used for queries is SQL (pronounced Sequel).

DataBase Management Systems

A DBMS is specialized software that enables the creation, update and query of databases. Small, but useful relational databases can be created on Windows PCs using Microsoft Access. (Some people use Microsoft Excel to create and manage personal databases). Industrial-strength applications call for powerful DBMS like Oracle (from Oracle, Inc), or SqlServer from Microsoft. The last two are full featured but tend to be expensive. MySQL is a free relational DBMS.

Applications that require very fast access and update of data represent another category of databases. Examples include airline reservation systems. Note that a major airline may need to make its entire reservations system available worldwide, updated and accurate 24 hours a day every day! This requires enormous effort and sophisticated programming.

It can be stated, without a trace of exaggeration, that without databases the modern world would not exist and computers would remain toys. The ability to store and access information, including non-numeric data, elevated computing from the level of mere calculators. The world-wide-web achieved its great success and ubiquity as soon as it was integrated with 'back-end' databases, enabling us to buy books, clothes, airline tickets, hotel reservations and every conceivable item online.

Impact on Future Technologies

Databases are here to stay and will remain important forever. The simple relational database model has proved to be remarkable robust, serving a wide variety of data types. It is also here to stay. However, advanced database technologies are emerging that manage not just alpha-numeric data but also images, audio, video and combinations such as medical data files. Some of these topics will be explored later in this text.

Concept Reinforcement:

1. For centuries, the most common storage medium for information was paper, bound into books, or as sheets of paper organized into file cabinets. Identify and explain at least three benefits of modern computer disk storage over paper-based media.

2. Following up from #1, can you identify at least one reason why paper-based media may be superior to disk storage?

3. On paper design a simple relational database (one table will suffice, or more if you like) describing the books you have read in the last 5 years.

Section 2.5 – Current Processor Technology

Section Objective:

- Understand the significance of Current processor technology on the science of computing, and analyze their impact on future technologies

What is current processor technology?

To meet the ever escalating demand for computing of various types, research in developing better processors is proceeding at a rapid pace worldwide. Although specialized applications require the development of specialized processors, for the general computing market there are two broad streams of current development. One is concerned with enhancing the capabilities of general purpose desktop computing, including the coming generations of Personal computers, and the other with mobile computing, especially for small devices such as smart phones that integrate communications with computing. In the following, the term microprocessor and processor are used synonymously.

Multi-core processors

One exciting class of current processors is the multi-core processors. Here, a core corresponds to a complete CPU such as Intel's Pentium. Multi-core processors place two or more cores on a single chip. By doing so the benefits of parallel computing can be obtained without having to interconnect separate boxes. Simplifying, it is as though we took two off the shelf PCs, threw away everything except the processor from one of them and then mashed the two processors into a single box. The resultant would be a single PC with a dual core processor.

There are many potential benefits from multi-core processors. But first, why do we need to design such processors at all? The reason is that computers do not perform just one task at any given time. Instead, people usually have multiple processes going on. The computer may be running a word processor, a spreadsheet and connecting to the web at the same time. In the web connection, the system may be running email, may have multiple web sites open and there may be multiple instant messaging sessions. In addition, the user may be listening to music at the same time and watching a video.

In a single core processor, all of these go through only one CPU. The reason it works is that modern CPUs operate at high clock speeds (more 2 Ghz), and the system moves data and programs in and out of the CPU very fast. In a multi-core system, even better efficiency (called throughput) can be achieved by dedicating a core (or more) to each of these processes. (The process executed by each core is called a thread) Data and programs corresponding to any thread flow in and out of the dedicated core, and multiple processes can execute simultaneously, each within their own dedicated cores. The operating system is responsible for assigning threads to cores. Thus, a very high level of parallelism can be achieved. In addition, the processor could include one or more special purpose cores, designed specifically for music, video, digital signal processing and others.

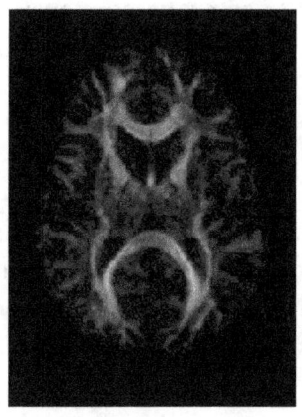

An MRI scan of a brain.

The need for multi-core processors also exists in many other applications. For example, in medical imaging, one single session in an MRI may generate a Terabyte of data. A terabyte is, 1 trillion bytes (10^{12}). Rapid processing of this amount of data is called Tera-scale computing, and while dual and quad-core processors are currently available, tera-scale computing is expected to require processors with 10 to 100 cores.

Many interesting and difficult computer science questions arise. One is how to interconnect all the cores so that, if needed, they can share data with each other within the processor. Another is how to do efficient load-sharing, i.e., how to find and send computing load from a busy processor to an idle one. An important related problem is hot spots, in which certain cores can get overheated due to excessive load while other parts of the chip are cool. On the software side, the operating system must know how to allocate specific processes to specific cores, and compute-intensive programs such as those used for sound and graphics may have to be rewritten to support parallelism. A processor-level technology for processing multiple threads in parallel is called hyper threading.

Mobile computing

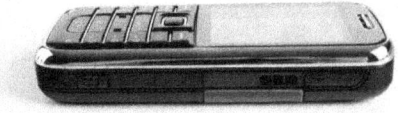

A close-up of a modern cell phone.

Cell phones, iPods, ever-smaller laptops, are examples of the explosion of mobile computing. The processors enabling mobile computing have special requirements on them. They must be light, draw as little power as possible, and dissipate very little heat. They should also be able to process wireless signals such as GPS and radio. Other functionality to be integrated is sensor data such as ambient temperature and humidity.

Mobile media players like the iPod use processors customized to enable efficient processing of music and video. General purpose processors like the Centrino, and Strong-ARM are used in laptops and PDAs.

Significance

The range of processor types for specialized applications and general-purpose computing is vast. There are specialized processors for video, audio, embedded computing, automobiles, and many others. Each application has its own set of requirements for power, speed, heat dissipation, reliability, and so on. Processors for satellites and space travel have to be designed to work flawlessly even in a high radiation environment including exposure to cosmic rays. Robotics calls for sensor integration, real-time mobility control, machine vision and many other concurrent processes. Each set of requirements calls for innovative computer science and engineering

Impact on Future Technologies

Each generation of processors builds upon experience and field usage to improve and develop better processors.

Concept Reinforcement:

1. Identify three other application areas for tera-scale computing.

2. What kinds of multi-processing does your brain perform?

3. What kinds of computing applications can *not* be parallelized?

Section 2.6 – Artificial Intelligence

Section Objective:

- Understand the significance of Artificial Intelligence on the science of computing, and analyze its impact on future technologies

What is Artificial Intelligence?

Artificial Intelligence (AI) is concerned with understanding intelligence and techniques for building machines that exhibit the properties commonly associated with intelligence. These properties include perception, situational awareness, language, advanced pattern recognition (like faces, smells, images) and all the many other features commonly associated with human and animal activities. It became apparent to computer scientists even in the 1950s, that such tasks, while definitely involving computation of some kind, are qualitatively different from the tasks computers are very good at doing. For example, repetitively carrying out numerical computations.

During these early years of computing and up to the early 1970s, as people began to realize what an amazing information-processing tool the computer represented, many extravagant predictions were made about the direction of computing. Reputable scientists felt that, apart from scientific number-crunching and calculations, computers would be able to understand natural languages, translate from one natural language to another (like French to Russian), do medical diagnoses, play chess at grand-master level, read handwriting, and many other similar activities.

However, by the late 1970s it became apparent that many of these hopes were too optimistic. While computers indeed made great strides in tackling not only scientific computations but also data bases, processing financial data, and managing vast amounts of information, there were certain tasks, such as the list above, that humans are very good at but computers are not. On the other hand, humans are not particularly good at doing accurately, and repeating consistently millions of times, all the other tasks that computers were good at.

Therefore, computer scientists realized a completely different kind of technology was needed if computers were to perform tasks that human intelligence excelled at. Such techniques were collectively named Artificial Intelligence, and research and development in this field became a major focus area of computing in the 1980s to the mid 1990s.

One important aspect of AI is knowledge representation, i.e., how to make computers 'understand' not only simple data like numbers and names but also much more complicated information. Consider visual perception. How do human brains perceive and memorize faces, shapes, patterns such as trees, clouds and so on? How can this kind of knowledge be converted into a form (the representation) that will help computers perform visual recognition, storage and search as well as brains do?

Several AI technologies have been developed by AI researchers. An early example is the Expert system. This consists of software, usually written in a special language called LISP (List Processor) that very often consisted of collections of rules. A typical rule consisted of a complicated 'if-then-else' construct, like 'If high fever then if stomach pain then if … else…".

Medical diagnosis was a popular topic for expert systems and systems like INTERNIST and MYCIN were developed. However, it became clear that rule-based expert systems suffer some significant defects. A major problem is that they are very brittle, in the sense that if even one clause of a long if-then-else is coded wrongly then major errors can result. In addition, the logic encoded in complex Boolean Logic rules is very hard for humans to write and to debug. Combinatorial explosion occurs in that the number of possible combinations of rules becomes very large (even up to thousands) very rapidly even for seemingly simple problems.

What was more, the question arose whether expert systems are really the way humans (and animals) reason and do computations in their brains. Therefore, some computer scientists started constructing software systems called neural nets. As the name implies, neural nets are a network of neuron-like software components. Each 'neuron' is associated with a number called its 'weight' and by clearly designing the (software) interconnections in the neural net scientists were able to develop neural nets that can recognize patterns. For example, long streams of text. Often, such software is trained by its users in a feedback process. Here, the software first reads the text and then produces what it thinks is the pattern. The programmers then adjust the weights and run it again, continuing until success is achieved on the text. This is often called supervised learning.

A simple neural network

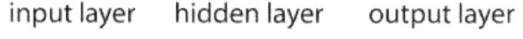
input layer   hidden layer   output layer

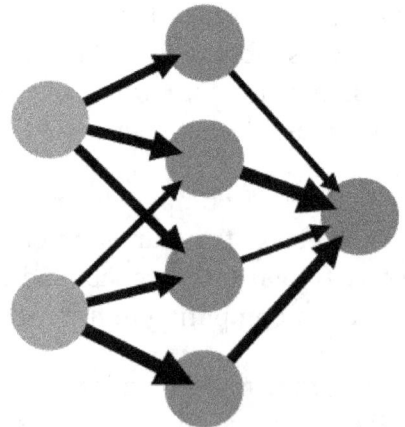

While neural nets are considered useful by many, other scientists are critical because neural nets cannot provide explanations of how they work and why they came to a particular conclusion. Also, they may need to be constantly retrained and adapted.

Significance

AI, or the attempt to do AI, has had enormous impact not only on computing, but also on diverse fields such as robotics, computer vision, medicine, games and others. Perhaps one of the greatest impacts is that it has led to a much greater appreciation of how complex information and knowledge can be and the capabilities of human (and animal) brains in processing these. With this realization many scientists realized that they needed to do fundamental research into cognition, i.e., the way brains perceive information, convert into internal knowledge representations and then perform intelligent activity.

At the same time, other groups of scientists continued to work intensively on more focused problems such as speech recognition, machine vision and similar problems. In these more restricted domains great strides have been made.

Impact on Future Technologies

Technologies that emulate intelligence will continue to improve and have great impact on future technologies that rely on computing. Examples include robotics, natural language processing, speech recognition. Recently one dream was realized when IBM's Deep Blue, and a chess-playing system, beat Gary Kasparov a chess grandmaster.

Concept Reinforcement:

1. Identify at least three attributes associated with intelligence.

2. Why is playing chess qualitatively different from number crunching?

3. Describe the significance of AI on fields other than computer science.

Section 2.7 – Operating Systems

Section Objective:

- Understand the significance of Operating Systems on the science of computing, and analyze its impact on future technologies

What is an Operating System?

Except for computers designed for very special and narrow purposes, every computer runs an operating system (OS). This is software that runs all the time, whenever a computer is on. Among its many functions, a very important one is to manage the flow of information across all the various components of a computer, both hardware and software. A typical data flow could be from hard disk to memory to the processor, then to a peripheral device like a printer, the display, or to a flash drive and so on. In addition, the processor is constantly executing instructions from any running programs (like games) and sending out requests for data. The OS ensures that all data is obtained from and sent to the right place and sent to the right place at the right time.

The OS is not just one program but a collection of programs (or subsystems) working together. These are often called systems programs in contrast to the many applications programs that a computer can run. An example of a systems program is the display subsystem that manages how text and graphics appear on the screen. Examples of application programs include a Word processor like Microsoft Word, graphics software like Photoshop, games like the Sims and so on.

An OS performing various tasks.

Why is an OS needed

The main function of a computer is to help people perform information processing tasks like writing documents, creating graphics, doing number crunching etc. These programs can be very complex to write, even for the most expert programmers. If these programmers had to also take care of the minute 'low-level' details of how to put dots and curves of different colors on the screen, or to read data from disk and send it to the processor, their task would multiply a hundred times or more in complexity and the time taken to do so would be increased by a hundred times or more! Instead the programming language used to write the application will have English-like commands for writing text in a particular color or font to the screen (or printer). These instructions (after being compiled) are then issued from the processor to the OS which executes all the low level details and accomplishes the task. In this way applications programmers are free to concentrate on improving the programs they are writing, making their games more interesting, give the paint program more features, and so on.

The OS performs many other tasks also. For instance, modern computers do not run just one application program at a time. Instead, most computers these days perform multi-tasking in which several applications programs are running at the same time. While creating a book report you may be simultaneously running a word processor, a web browser (like Mozilla Firefox), a paint program, and also listening to music from your computer's DVD player. The computer may also have instant messaging turned on and is constantly watching for messages to show up.

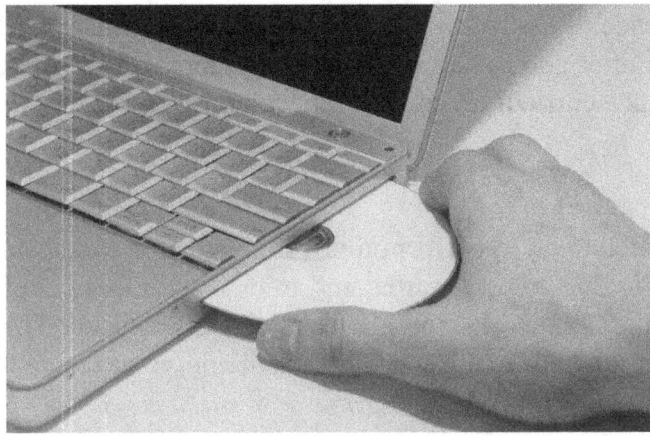

A dvd being inserted into a laptop.

The data and instructions for all these programs go through a CPU and from the disk system to memory to display to audio to the networking connection and so on. It is the OS that choreographs this intricate dance and makes sure that all these different kinds of information don't end up crashing into each other, ensuring that a data stream meant for the paint program doesn't end up in the word processor, or that music data intended for the computer's audio output doesn't end up on the screen!

Other operating systems, like UNIX are designed to allow not just multi-tasking but multiple users to be running their own programs. These multi-user operating systems have to also manage the workload of numerous users who 'log-in' to the computer and logout as they choose.

The OS does these and a host of other tasks that enable its users, to execute their desired applications smoothly. Since many of its functions relate very closely to the hardware of the computer, including the processor(s), operating systems are usually written for specific processors. The Windows OS is specific to the Intel x86 family of microprocessors. However, Windows is not the only OS that has been written for this microprocessor family. There are versions of LINUX, and recently, the Macintosh OS was written to run on x86 processors.

Yet another 'multi' managed and enabled by modern Operating Systems is multi-processing. Here, the computer has not one but many processors. Such parallel and distributed computer systems are used to perform huge tasks, such as creating animation movies like 'Madagascar.' In such systems, every task is split into many smaller tasks that are then assigned with the help of the OS to available processors. In such systems the OS can also be tasked with load sharing, in which the OS constantly searches for lightly loaded processors and moves tasks from highly loaded ones to the lightly loaded ones. This increases efficiency and reduces the time it takes to complete the major tasks.

Significance

The Operating System is an indispensable component of any modern computer. By freeing applications programmers from having to deal with the low-level details of the computer hardware, a great burst of creativity arose leading to the sophisticated programs that we take for granted today. Instead of writing their programs for a specific processor or for a collection of hardware, people write for a specific operating system, knowing that no matter what the underlying hardware is, they can expect their applications to behave as expected. Advances in the science of OS led to multi-tasking and multi-use capabilities, thus greatly expanding the capabilities and functionality of computers. OS continues to be a major part of the computer science curriculum and an important area of research.

Impact on Future Technologies

As computers get called upon to perform more sophisticated tasks, such as managing networks of computers to operate in parallel, and to deal with more sophisticated peripheral devices, the role of the OS, and its complexity, will only expand. This will apply specifically to computing in specialized areas such as medicine, robotics, mobile phones and others.

Concept Reinforcement:

1. Explain the difference between systems and applications programming

2. How does the OS enable the same application to execute on different kinds of hardware.

3. Explain the difference between multi-tasking and multi-user operating systems. Is a multi-tasking OS necessarily a multi-user OS?

Section 2.8 – Computer Architecture

Section Objective:

- Understand the significance of Computer Architecture on the science of computing, and analyze their impact on future technologies

What is Computer Architecture?

Computer Architecture (CA) is concerned with the assembly and interconnection of hardware components to build computing equipment for specific design and performance objectives. It is an important branch of computer science and engineering.

The term 'Architecture' in the context of computing can refer to both hardware and software architecture. In this chapter we will focus on the former. However, the topic is vast and the following few pages will only cover the bare outline.

Von Neumann Architecture

At a very basic level, all computers in general used today follow the von Neumann Architecture.

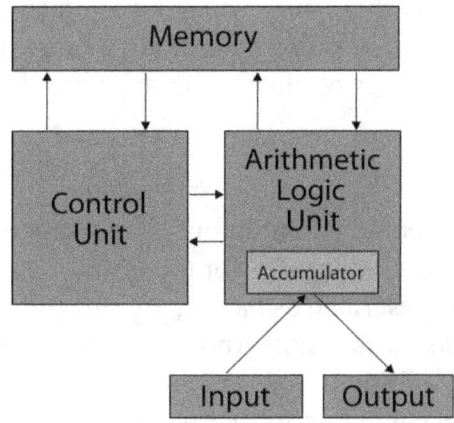

A diagram of von Neumann architecture.

This architecture shows a clear separation between the processor, the Arithmetic Logic Unit (ALU), the control unit, main memory, and Input/Output. The first three components are typically combined into a single entity, the CPU. The figure also illustrates the typical data flow in which the I/O subsystem exchanges data with the CPU and the latter in turn exchanges data with main memory. The I/O subsystem typically consists of disk storage, keyboard, network cards, video cards, the display(s), printers, and scanners. In personal computers (PCs) the CPU is the microprocessor, implemented as a single integrated circuit (IC). Main memory is also referred to as RAM. In addition, the CPU typically has a small amount of memory in hardware called registers.

The data flow between the I/O subsystem and the CPU is done by the system bus, or just bus.

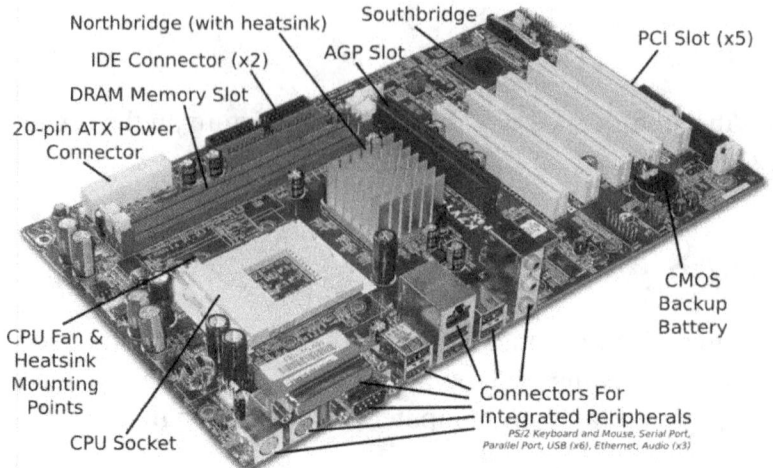

A motherboard with the components labeled courtesy of Moxfyre.

PCs implement all these components on a single printed circuit board, called the motherboard. The motherboard may have slots connected directly to the bus into which other boards can be slid. These can be network cards, video cards and so on. When a PC hardware manufacturer allows users to open out the case and attach third-party components to be inserted, the architecture of the system is said to be open. This is the case with most Windows PCs, to the extent that building a PC from off-the-shelf components is a form of entertainment to many. On the other hand, when a manufacturer does not allow such tinkering, the architecture is said to be closed. Most computers from Apple Corp. as well as PDAs and cell phones are examples of closed architectures.

System Clock

Note that computers do not operate in continuous time. Unlike a car, that is either stopped or rolling along smoothly, activity inside a computer occurs only when an internal clock beats. So, when a computer is described as having a 1 Ghz (Giga Hertz) processor, it means that its system clock (located on the motherboard) ticks one billion times every second. Putting it another way, every billionth of a second the CPU issues an instruction resulting in some kind of data flows in some part of the machine. The sheer speed makes its operation appear continuous. Some modern CPUS, are superscalar, i.e., they can issue more than one instruction, to different parts of the CPU in each clock cycle, thus achieving a form of instruction-level parallel processing.

Also, even though most PCs have only one central processor, there may be other microprocessors performing specialized tasks. For example, many video cards are themselves computers that are focused on taking in video data in the form of streams of 0s and 1s and converting into instructions for painting the display. These may not operate at the rate of the main CPU clock speed; but will typically operate at fractional multiples that still enable synchronization.

CA has a very close relationship to computer performance analysis, a highly quantitative way of describing how well a computer works. Some parameters that go into this are the clock speed, the word length of the CPU, the word length of the bus, the speed of the bus, the amount of RAM, the size of the cache, the number of caches, the amount of memory on the video card, the number of colors on the display, the dot size, and many others. Here, the word length is the maximum number of bits that the CPU can process at any one time. Typically it is expressed in multiples of 8 with most current processors having 32 bit word lengths. The higher the word length the more information (program instructions and data) the CPU can process simultaneously. When applied to the bus, the word length is the maximum number of bits the bus can handle at any instant.

RAM, is of course, Random Access Memory (main memory) and it is the amount of memory available as a scratch pad for the CPU. Greater amounts of RAM means that larger amounts of information can remain close to the CPU. The cache is special high speed memory in between the CPU and main memory in which the system stores information that may be immediately needed by the CPU. There is a memory hierarchy in most computers in terms of speed of access from the CPU. The fastest are the registers, located inside the IC comprising the CPU. These are followed by cache(s), RAM, and disk storage, in order of decreasing speed.

Developing the architecture for a new computer usually starts out with requirements on its eventual cost, power consumption, performance parameters and similar. The job of the architects is to devise a mix of components, including interconnections, to meet the requirements. They may also have to devise ways to ensure heat dissipation since computers operating at high clock speeds also tend to emit heat.

Components of Computer Architecture

A video card isolated on white.

Also, apart from the selection of the various components (CPU, video card etc) there are some 'lower-level' aspects to architecture. Two of these are the Instruction Set Architecture (ISA), which is the design of the kinds of instructions that the CPU can accept and process, and the microarchitecture (also known as computer organization) which is the designed assembly of 'low-level' components like the gates, microcontrollers and similar. An interesting example of an ISA is RISC, which stands for Reduced Instruction Set Computing. RISC was devised after computer scientists realized that for many contexts, it was better to design the CPU to process a few simple instructions very well and very fast, rather than to build in the complexity needed to perform numerous complicated and lengthy instructions (CISC, Complex Instruction Set computing).

The final performance of a computer is a very complicated function of many factors. For example, a computer with a 64 bit processor may function slower than a 32 bit processor if the bus in the former only allows 16 bit words. Also, performance is highly dependent on the kind of task being performed. A computer designed for playing games may be quite unsuitable as a database server. A computer with the highest rated components may have poor performance if its instruction set of its CPU is designed inefficiently.

Significance

CA is the core of computer science and engineering. Research and development of sophisticated algorithms for ISAs, techniques such as caching, RISC, and hundreds of others have contributed immensely to the field.

Impact on Future Technologies

CA has been, and will be an intensely exciting and complicated subject. As people demand more and more from computing, such as smaller phones, personalized robots, the ability to perform in extreme environments, virtual reality, and numerous others, its impact in the future will only increase. It is well worth repeating that the above few pages have barely scratched the surface of CA.

Concept Reinforcement:

1. Explain the role of the clock in a computer.

2. What are the benefits of the von Neumann architecture? What possible limitations could it place on future computing?

3. What are some reasons why higher clock speeds do not necessarily indicate better overall performance?

Section 2.9 – Computer Graphics

Section Objective:

- Understand the significance of computer graphics on the science of computing, and analyze its impact on future technologies

What is computer graphics?

Computer graphics (CG) refers to the use of the computer to create and manipulate pictorial content. It is closely related to computer animation. We will discuss mostly static images in this section.

Except for the very high-end, expensive ones, early computer systems included monitors and printers that could support only characters, by the mid 1980s the emergence of color bit-mapped displays, the mouse pointer, high quality color printers led scientists to the realization that high quality images could also be created and manipulated using computer hardware and software. This led to an enormous outpouring of creativity in both hardware and software, with advances in each field motivating and inspiring the other. On the hardware side the main advances were in the sophistication of displays and video cards, On the software side were algorithms and programs that gave the graphic artist a huge variety of visual effects to work with.

Display characteristics

The resolution of any display medium refers to the smallest size dot that can be written (addressed). In computer displays, people speak of the pixel, short for picture element. The properties of a pixel that can be controlled are its color and brightness and these can be set by the number of bits that can be used to address it. Clearly, the larger the number of pixels for a fixed screen size, the higher the resolution. In an 8 bit display, each pixel could have 256 levels of brightness, resulting in 256 levels of gray on non-color displays. On color displays, each pixel consists of 3 components, one each for Red, Green and Blue. By controlling the brightness of each, a 24 bit display (also called a True color display) can yield up to 16 million colors from each pixel.

CG Software

The purpose of CG software is to enable the easy creation of a range of visual effects. When displays had low resolution, one area of research was how to draw lines (straight and otherwise), that didn't appear jagged. Nowadays, more sophisticated issues arise that use complicated mathematics such as splines, Bezier curves and similar.

CG comes in two flavors: 2-D and 3-D. The former leads to 'flat' images while the latter provides depth, distance, complex lighting, true shadows, and so on. 3-D turns out to be much more complicated than 2-D. The famous Rubik's cube puzzle is said to have been invented by Professor Rubik for the purpose of illustrating to his students how much more complex 3-D is than 2-D.

A slim robot rendered in CG.

Essentially, CG software is based on mathematical algorithms. These support the creation of effects such as transparency (to varying degrees), lighting, shadows, reflections, textures, and a host of others. In addition, CG software often supports rotation, zooming, twisting, deformation, and many other image manipulation options.

Images need not, of course, be developed solely on the computer. The development of high-resolution scanning hardware enables print photographs (sometimes from the original film), to be imported into the computer and manipulated by programs such as PhotoShop in a process called image processing.

The process of depicting a final image on the screen, complete with colors and all the visual effects desired, is called rendering. This can be very compute-intensive, taking large amounts of time and memory, depending on the size and complexity of the image.

Saving images

A typical image can, depending on its resolution, take enormous amounts of memory to manipulate and store. Special formats, called image formats have been developed for the purpose of saving images to disk for later retrieval. Formats such as JPEG (also JPG), GIF, are said to be lossy, because some image resolution is lost for the sake of saving disk space. Others such as TIFF, EPS, BMP, preserve all details of the original image.

Image data compression is an active area of research. An early technique is called run-length encoding. Here, if an image has a stream of, say yellow dots, instead of 'writing out' each dot, the count of yellow dots is written out.

Significance

CG has had great impact on computing hardware and software technologies. It enabled a large group of creative people, not just artists, to make use of the technology and gave rise to a new medium. On the hardware side, CG spurred the development of better displays, video cards, specialized graphics processors, vast amounts of disk storage packed into ever smaller physical sizes, faster memory and so on. On the software side, CG led to algorithms and programs that could help the user create complex images that would otherwise require great skills in handling paint and brush. Of course, this does not mean that CG does not require artistic ability to create pleasing images!

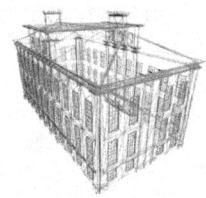

A CAD rendering of a building.

The applications of CG are not just in the arts. Engineers rely heavily on CG to produce detailed engineering and architectural drawings. This is known as CAD (Computer Aided Design) supported by commercial software such as AutoCAD. It is now increasingly common for architects and engineers to do collaborative work across continents using specialized CAD systems. A benefit of using CG and CAD is that the images can be rotated, zoomed, twisted, viewed from multiple angles, and manipulated in real time enabling engineers to even do complex simulations. For example, architects can simulate walking through a proposed building. An entire discipline called scientific visualization enables the pictorial rendering and manipulation of complex mathematical functions, statistical data, and physical entities. This can be very useful for teaching and to gain insights into the phenomena being visualized and modeled.

Apart from professionals of various kinds, all of computing has benefited from CG since it has improved the appearance of displays, made computing seem much more friendly, and enabled the Graphical User interface (GUI).

Impact on Future Technologies

Many scientists believe that we are still in the babyhood of CG. The future developments (apart from more sophisticated animation) already include so-called Virtual Reality and immersive environments in which the user is placed inside a synthetic environment that has elements of reality. Systems like "Second Life" are examples.

Concept Reinforcement:

1. Explain how a 24 bit display can yield about 16 million colors per pixel.

2. How does CG enable development of better user interfaces?

Section 2.10 – Computer Animation

Section Objective:

- Understand the significance of computer animation on the science of computing, and analyze its impact on future technologies

What is computer animation?

Computer Animation (CGA) refers to the use of computers to create, edit, and manipulate moving images. Because computer graphics (CG) is the basis of computer animation we shall speak of animation using computers as CGA.

The reason animation works is the persistence of vision in the human optical system. Because an image remains in the eye and in the brain for a small amount of time, a succession of very similar still images is perceived as continuous motion provided the images go by at least at 14 images per second. In fact most modern animation uses 24 to 30 images per second. Hence, if CG places great demands on computing systems and peripherals, CGA places even more demands.

Traditionally, animation was done by artists who painstakingly drew and colored a series of pictures that differed very slightly from the previous one. At the minimum rate of 14 images (frames) per second, each minute of animation needs 840 frames. Clearly, great skill is needed to develop believable, smooth motion. In addition, the motion must be synchronized to music (if any). Typically the animation is tailored to the beat and tempo of the music rather than the other way around.

Professional quality movies need 24 frames/second, so that 1440 images must be drawn and painted for each minute. Often, the main creative artists in an animation movie drew the beginning and end of a particular motion, leaving the in-between to others. Once the frames had been drawn and colored they were transferred to reel film by means of special stop-motion animation cameras. Further, most hand-drawn cartoons are 2-D, leading to a flat appearance. Doing true 3-D animation by hand is very difficult.

A 3D rendering of an apartment.

In the 1980s a few pioneers saw the potential of computing to create animations. Their research influenced the development of a new discipline within computer science, namely computer graphics and animation (CGA). This relies heavily on complex mathematics and creative software programming to develop techniques for automatic in-betweening, 3-D motion, morphing, lighting, and many special motion effects. The computer can do most of these better than humans can. For example, truly smooth motion, in part by going up to 30 frames/second, is enabled by mathematical algorithms and clever programming. Note that it is not enough for the programs to work; they must work quickly and efficiently to be usable in near real-time by animators.

This is not to say that animation is easier or less time consuming than when done manually. Rather, the capabilities of computing, and the ever-growing expectations of audiences mean that CG animators are constantly under pressure to come up with better, more realistic, more complex products. Some software to help create sophisticated animations includes MAYA and 3D-Studio Max.

Another interesting aspect is that CGA is now the basis of not one, but at least two big industries. For most of the last 100 years, animation and the movies have been intimately linked. With the advent of computing machinery, animation, specifically CGA, is also the basis for another industry, games. By some measures games are currently a bigger industry than Hollywood.

Games put even greater pressure on the computing system and the animation since they are interactive, and the computer must respond instantly in real-time to the player's responses and commands. Specialized game playing computers (like the Playstation™ and Xbox™) are currently used.

Significance

CGA has motivated the advancement of computing in many ways since it places great challenges on the technology. These demands led to great advances in computing hardware and software. For instance, computer scientists figured out how to encode the basic 3-D CGA software and algorithms into integrated chips. Such chips are much faster than executing the same software in a conventional computer system.

An animated mechanical droid.

Creating the final frame of a professional quality animation movie, or one that mixes live action and CGA, poses extreme computing challenges. The final frames have to be of extremely high resolution if they are to appear in smooth rich color on a huge movie screen, not just a small display. The problem is even more challenging for IMAX movies. This process, called rendering, requires enormous amounts of computing time, memory, storage, and hardware and is often done on so-called render farms. Typically, a render farm consists of large numbers of computers linked together and sharing the job. The underlying technologies of parallel and distributed computing, load-sharing and similar, were motivated by the needs of CGA.

In addition, it should be emphasized, that CGA is not just visuals. Audio processing, to meet the needs of movies and games has also made great advances such as digital audio, synthesizers, audio editors and similar.

Impact on Future Technologies

CGA is very likely to impact future Research and development in computing. Immersive games and movie environments are being imagined by some scientists and artists. These will require more sophisticated algorithms, hardware and software.

Concept Reinforcement:

1. At 30 frames/second, how many frames are needed for a fully animated 2 hour feature film?

2. Why is rendering the final animation so compute intensive?

3. Apart from games and entertainment movies, in what other activities can CGA make an impact?

Section 2.11 – Computer Security

Section Objective:

- Understand the significance of computer security on the science of computing, and analyze its impact on future technologies

What is Security?

A picture of a padlock sitting on a laptop keypad.

Security in the context of computing refers to preventing unauthorized access to the data and programs that you own, or are responsible for. In addition, it refers also to protecting your computers from being taken over, corrupted, or damaged (with respect to software).

Unfortunately, as computing has become increasingly ubiquitous, and the information that people store on their computers becomes ever more valuable, there are plenty of people who make great attempts to attack other people's computers, i.e., commit a form of cyber-crime. Some do it purely as an exploit to brag about. Others attack in order to gain personal information to commit, for example, identity theft. The computer systems of large corporations are attacked by those seeking industrial knowledge. The military's systems are constantly under attack by cyber-spies. All of these people are actively engaged in seeking vulnerabilities in computer systems and devising ways to exploit these for their own unsavory reasons.

Computer networking, in particular, connecting to the internet enables a very large proportion of attacks. A stand-alone computer, kept under lock and key, is much more secure than one connected 24 hours of the day to the internet and not protected by special security software. However, even computers isolated from the internet need to be protected. This is because in any organization, access to information has to be kept controlled. Not all employees of a company should have access to medical or personal information (in the human resources department) of other employees. In addition, non-employees should definitely not have any but the most minimal level of access.

For this reason almost all computers are protected by a username/password combination. There are weak passwords and strong passwords. Weak passwords are those that are of short length (6 characters or less) and the characters are just letters and numbers with no distinction between upper and lower case. Examples of strong passwords are those required to consist of 10 or more case-sensitive letters, numbers, special characters (like $, %) and are also required to change every two months.

For a criminal to break into someone else's password protected account, both the username and password must be known. Usernames are often easy to get, especially since they form part of people's email addresses. Cracking a strong password can be very difficult and in addition, many systems freeze out access attempts after a small number of incorrect tries.

For this reason, some people use social engineering to get access to computer systems. This may consist of persuading someone with access to give out his/her access information. The persuasion has taken forms like bribes, blackmail, romantic promises and similar. Note that in highly sensitive contexts like hospitals, an employee can be terminated for revealing their password(s) to anyone else, even a co-worker.

Computer systems can be isolated, while still allowing access to the internet, by means of software intensive hardware called firewalls, placed directly between the computer system and its connection to the public internet. Firewalls can scan every incoming data packet and deny access from the outside to all but a trusted set of outside computers. Similarly, they can block access to specific external web sites from within the system.

Security Model

The netBSD screen running on a UNIX computer.

The security model of a system refers to the way in which access rights to programs and data are given to particular users and administrators. This is especially important in multi-user operating systems such as UNIX and its variants. Here, every file and program can have three levels of read, write, and execute access. The main systems administrator, called root, has all 3 levels of access for all programs and data. A user that creates a file or a program typically is given all three levels and can share a combination of these rights/privileges with his/her group. So, if you create a file then you can designate a collection of your friends that can read and write to the file but public users (other than root) can only read the file. On the other hand, access to many systems functions, such as the allocation of disk space, is only done by root or persons designated by root. Because root can do anything to the system, a prized goal of hackers (people that try to gain unauthorized access to a system) is to get root access.

The vulnerability of computing systems to security attacks has led to advances in the science of technology of protection. In particular methods of encrypting data such as the contents of computer storage, or information emailed across the internet, have become ever more sophisticated. A common method of ensuring data security is called the RSA algorithm which is an implementation of Public Key Encryption (PKE). The basis of PKE is that there are certain mathematical functions that are easy to apply to a number, thus resulting in encryption, but very hard to reverse, i.e., to decrypt. An example of such a function is to factor a very large number into prime factors.

To prevent data being stolen during transmission over the web, some sites that may take financial information are set up as secure sites and the URL must be accessed using not http but https. The technology behind this is also a from of automatics PKE.

Virtual Private Networks were developed to protect computer systems while allowing some access from the outside to trusted users only. In recent times, biometric protection methods are becoming more common. One can buy hardware and software that reads a fingerprint and enables access to a system only if that fingerprint is applied to the hardware sensor.

Impact on Future Technologies

Security is a vast topic and here we have barely scratched the surface. We haven't covered, for example, viruses, worms, Trojan horses, spam, bots, and other nasty mal-ware.

Unfortunately, cyber crime and attacks on computing systems show no sign of abating. Some governments are themselves suspected of sponsoring cyber-espionage, especially on the United States. Thus, the need for security measures will only increase. The US government is said to begin requiring that the contents of all computers it owns should be encrypted, especially laptops used by traveling officials.

Security is also an issue for ordinary folks. Nowadays, one cannot let a computer be connected to the internet even for a few minutes without first installing security software that checks to see whether any incoming data looks like mal-ware. An active area of research is to find methods to detect incoming spam mail.

A woman enjoying wireless internet access on her laptop.

Wireless networks pose particular challenges because anyone within range can receive the wireless signals. WEP encryption is used to prevent so-called parking lot attacks in which hackers sit in their cars on the parking lot of a company and read all the wireless traffic. As the computing capability of cell phones continues to increase the need for security to protect these will also become important.

Concept Reinforcement:

1. Explain what is a security model.

2. Why is a strong password harder to crack than a weak one?

3. What are the implications on your personal privacy if others gain access to your computer?

Section 2.12 – Software Engineering

Section Objective:

- Understand the significance of Software Engineering on the science of computing, and analyze its impact on future technologies

What is Software Engineering?

Software Engineering (SE) is the science and technology of developing good software, i.e., computer programs that are error (bug)-free, have good user interfaces, and are well documented, extensible, scalable, among other desirable attributes. Software that is properly engineered can be expected to perform well, satisfy the needs of its users, and be a significant asset to the enterprise. On the other hand, software that has many bugs, does not address user's needs cannot easily be changed to meet changing needs, can cause economic damage to its owners.

Let us now see what some of these terms mean.

Error (bug) – free

A picture of a bug on a computer board.

Legend has it that when computers were big hulking metallic boxes occupying large rooms, a programmer trying to find out why his program was not working correctly opened up one of the boxes and saw a dead insect inside it. He or she attributed the error to the bug and from then on, programs that had errors were described as having bugs.

Bugs arise for many reasons. Those that are caused by misspelling a word of the programming language being used are easily caught by the compiler. Others, related to program logic, i.e., the way the program is written, can be much more subtle to find and can only be located after extensively testing the program against all possible combinations of input data. This process is called Quality Assurance (QA). Software companies typically have QA groups, or contract with external companies. The person(s) who wrote the program cannot adequately perform QA because he/she has a mind-set that prevents testing the program against all possible data inputs and program conditions. You may have noticed that others who read something you have written (like a book report) can find spelling mistakes and logical inconsistencies much better than you can.

A buggy program exhibits a number of undesirable behaviors. It could crash, i.e., end unexpectedly making you lose all the work you have done, or hang, i.e., go into a non-responsive frozen state. It could give obvious errors such as calculating the wrong final price for your purchases. In a sense, these kinds of bugs are much better than those in which the program provides erroneous output but these errors are not immediately obvious. Such bugs can be very hard to detect and correct.

Extensible

Software is described as extensible if it has been written in such a way that new functions can easily be added to it. This is an important property because a) it is very hard to anticipate well in advance what new functions and features will be needed, and b) most software is released in versions, with each version having more features, or improved implementations of old ones.

Scalable

Software that can process large increases in the amount of input data without getting slowed down excessively, is said to be scalable. This is particularly important for multi-user software such as a web-site. There have been instances where a web site running perfectly well became overwhelmed by a sudden influx of users and then crashed. While scalability can be aided by use of powerful hardware, it is also important to write the programs in such a way as to enhance scalability.

Well-documented

Software is said to be well-documented if its design, functionality, the way it is written, changes, user-interface, screens, etc have been described and documented in sufficient detail so that a new programmer joining the team can read the material and understand the inner details of the software rapidly. In addition, documentation should also be present in the program code itself by adding comment lines in the code that are not processed by the compiler but reside at appropriate locations within the program code. These can explain why the programmer chose to do the program logic in the way displayed. Another aid to readers of the program is to make the variable names descriptive. A program variable name like 'Gender_of_Study_Subject' is much more meaningful than 'XYZ.'

Note that documentation is not just for those who didn't write the program code. Each and every programmer has had the unpleasant experience of writing what seems like very obvious and transparent code only to find out as soon as two days later, that he/she cannot recall why he/she wrote those lines!!

User Interface

The user interface (UI) is the way in which users interact with the software. This is what users see and experience and how they form their impressions of the software. Therefore, the UI must not only have attractive screens, easy to understand instructions, avoid duplicate data entry, and so on, but must also know the mental model(s) of the intended user group(s). For example, the same information about a disease must be presented very differently to physicians as to lay persons.

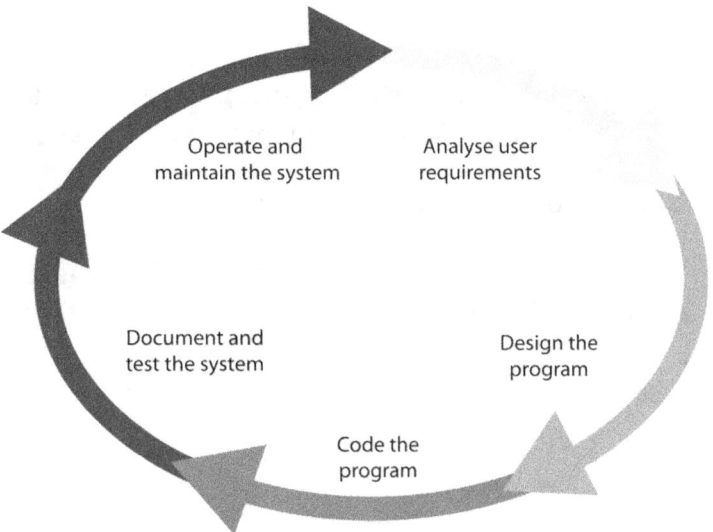

An example of a software dev cycle.

The software development life cycle (SDLC) refers to a structured process of creating software. The following is very brief outline. The first step is usually to create a requirements document that describes in a very detailed way what the software is required to do, what kind of input data it must handle and so on. The next step is the functional specifications that describe what functions the software will perform, including screen designs, to meet the requirements. Next comes the Software Architecture, i.e., the list of software modules, and the way they will interact. This can be followed by detail design. Coding then starts and after a sufficient code-base, has been developed it can be sent for initial Quality Assurance where bugs are identified. These are assigned to the programmer(s) and sent to QA again after they have been fixed. After a certain point the software is deemed ready for production, also known as release.

Significance

It is easy to write programs that, even though they may have complicated functionality, are intended only for personal use. It is very difficult to write software that is intended for large numbers of other people. Software intended for public use, needs to be developed by large teams of programmers, is required to have industrial-strength reliability, and is expected to be used for years to come. Software engineering is what enables the last two and transformed programming from a hobby to a truly industrial process that is now the foundation of the multi-trillion dollar worldwide software industry. In a very real sense SE has created the modern world of computing, including all the web sites that we find we cannot function without.

Impact on Future Technologies

As the world comes to depend even more heavily on computers, the importance of SE can only increase. Now applications of computing such as medical robotics may demand even more sophisticated and stringent SE techniques.

Concept Reinforcement:

1. Identify some specific software, like a web site, that you consider to have a good user interface. Analyze and explain why you regard it to be good.

2. What is the difference between extensibility and scalability?

3. What are some reasons why writing software for public use takes much more effort than the same functionality for personal use.

Section 2.13 – Computer Networking

Section Objective:

- Understand the significance of computer networking on the science of computing, and analyze its impact on future technologies

What is Computer Networking?

The science and technology of connecting computers and peripheral devices such as printers, so that they can share data, programs, and functionality is called computer networking, or simply networking. Of course, data communications underlies all of networking. An important concept here is that computers send data to each other in the form of a sequence of 0s, and 1s. called a packet.

Types of Networks

There are several ways of classifying networks. A common one is by scale, in other words, the geographic span of the network. A home network is usually anywhere from 2 to 10 computers and one or more printers. A Local Area Network may span an office or a large laboratory or a building. A wide area network may be spread across an entire college campus or even a city. Of course the Internet spans the widest area, namely the whole world!

Networks may also be classified according to their topology, i.e., the way they are interconnected to each other as defined by the interconnection graph. Some network topologies are ring, star, mesh and so on. This classification seems to be more appropriate to LANs. The reasons for selecting a particular topology are related to cost, physical constraints and so on. Note that topology is not necessarily determined by the physical cabling, but by how the networking software enables computers in a network to see each other. It is quite possible to make a physically connected computer in a network inaccessible to any other.

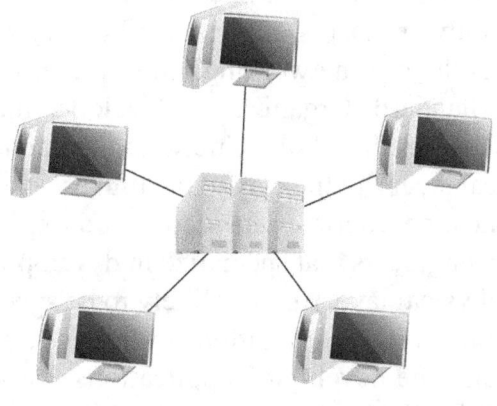

Star Topology.

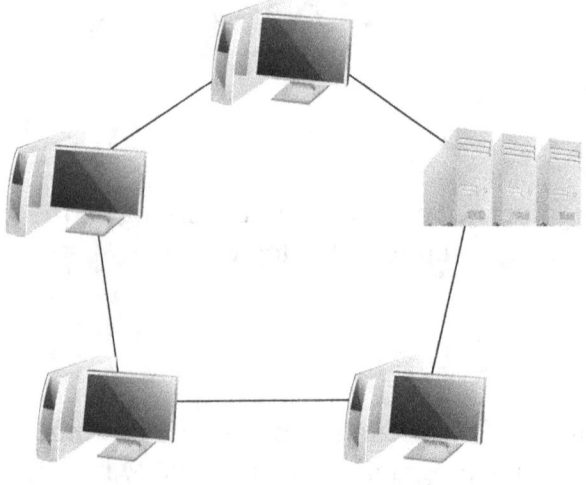

Ring Topology.

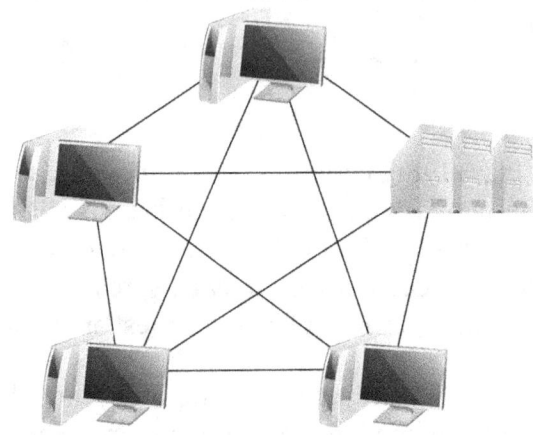

Mesh topology.

Networking Technology

Networking is a topic of great interest to computer scientists and engineers at all levels from the basics of cabling or wireless communications, to data communications protocols, networking hardware, the software that is implemented by networking hardware, and useful applications that can result from networking. Due to the inherent complexity of networking, the International Standards Organization developed the Open Systems Interconnect reference model. This divides the whole of networking into layers (see Figure) moving from the lowest (the Physical layer) all the way to the highest (the applications layer). Such layering ensures that the most appropriate knowledge and experience are brought to bear on each layer. For example, engineers that specialize in developing better fiber optic cables and fiber optic hardware (physical layer) are not likely to be specialists in developing web-based software (Applications layer). In addition, by specifying standards and protocols that are accepted by all, someone developing applications can work at that level without worrying about lower level details that have been taken care of, and standardized by other experts.

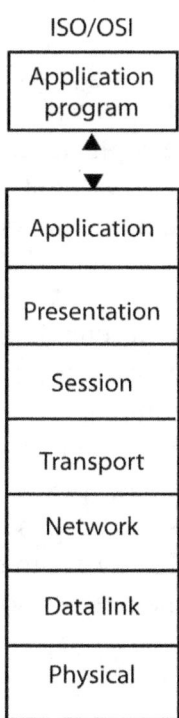

ISO/OSI

| Application program |
| Application |
| Presentation |
| Session |
| Transport |
| Network |
| Data link |
| Physical |

Networking Hardware

Networks are implemented using specialized hardware. At the physical layer we are concerned with cables and wireless technologies. LANs can often be implemented using wireless, in which case each computer needs a wireless network adapter whose function is to pick up a wireless signal and convert it into a form suitable for use by the computer. Wireless routers broadcast data signals. Their range is usually limited to about 100 feet. This technology is called WiFi.

Wired networks rely on Network Interface Cards at each computer connected by means of CAT 5 or CAT 6 cables. Data signals travel across cables through several hardware devices before reaching their destination. Some of these devices are the following

Routers are software intensive devices that examine each incoming packet's header for the destination address and then send the packet on to another location based on routing tables that specify the addresses of the best route(s) to the final desired destination.

Repeaters take an incoming signal, pump energy into it and send it on. They are needed because over long distances digital signals tend to attenuate (ie lose power).

Hubs connect different networks together to make them look like one.

Firewalls are devices that protect an organizations network from entry of packets from undesirable locations. More sophisticated than routers, the software of a firewall examines each incoming packet and then applies rules set by the organization to prevent or allow the packets from entering.

In addition, firewalls can also regulate the destination of packets sent out from the organizations network.

Networking Software

Software plays a very big role in networking at several levels. Important networking devices like routers and firewalls are software intensive. Other software, like web servers and browsers enable the web and web-based applications. Security software ensures the protection of personal data. This is especially important for wireless networking since wireless signals are broadcast and can be picked up by anyone in range. Wired Equivalent Privacy (WEP) is often used in this context.

One important benefit of networking is to enable the power of distributed computing in which networked computers work together, sharing resources including memory and processors to solve large problems. Supercomputers are typically developed nowadays by networking together hundreds of computers each relatively cheap. These computers may not share memory, but communicate by message passing. Large and complex computing tasks can be broken down into smaller pieces and each is handled by one of the computers in the network. All this is managed by special software to ensure load sharing (in which computers distribute computing load among themselves so none gets overworked), coordination of processors/resources, and others.

Significance

Networking can be considered the most significant leap in computing since the invention of the computer itself. The Internet and the world-wide web have enabled such amazing distance-shrinking technologies such as web-based video conferencing, collaboration applications, access to worldwide knowledge resources and information banks, instant messaging, chat, and many others. Grid computing extends the distributed computing model from beyond a LAN to, in principle, the entire internet.

Essentially, the main significance of networking is that it enables computing tasks to be extended and shared from one computer to potentially hundreds others. This is the meaning of the saying "The network is the computer."

Impact on Future Technologies

Networking will only increase in sophistication and impact. An emerging technology called Wimax can enable wireless data communications over an entire city. Access to the internet is available by means of cell phone technology on devices such as Blackberries and smart phones. Of course, accessing the internet requires rather sophisticated browsers, and processors powerful enough to execute the software. However, an interesting development is called dust networking. Here, each 'computer' is basically a sensor equipped with wireless communications hardware and also a small low power processor. The main function of these is to constantly monitor environmental parameters like temperature, humidity, chemical concentrations, and transmit the data. TinyOS is an operating system designed specifically for such networks. One interesting feature is that they can self-organize themselves into a network and be robust enough to continue even a few become inactive. Such wireless sensor networks are extremely valuable in industrial settings. NASA uses these in the space shuttle to monitor temperatures across the surface. They could eventually lead to ubiquitous computing.

Concept Reinforcement:

1. How does distributed computing enable people to do large computing tasks?

2. Explain and expand on the statement "The network *is* the computer".

3. What is the role of a repeater in a network?

Section 2.14 – Human Computer Interaction

Section Objective:

- Understand the significance of human computer interaction on the science of computing, and analyze its impact on future technologies

What is human computer interaction?

Very broadly speaking Human Computer Interaction (HCI) refers to the ways in which humans use computers, how information and commands are given to computers and how they are received back by humans.

From a science and technology point of view, HCI includes both hardware devices and also software, especially in the form of user interfaces.

At the very dawn of the computer era, in the 1950s, computers were programmed mostly by changing the physical wiring of the computer's components. Thankfully, this was soon replaced by stored-program computers in which, as we have seen, the program was typed in a programming language and then stored digitally on a storage medium (disk or tape). Note that at this point the only human interacting with computers were programmers and they tolerated quite a bit of awkwardness and difficulties in their interactions.

However, as computer began to be used by non-programmers such as data entry operators, and even later, by ordinary users, the topic of HCI acquired great scientific significance and is now an important discipline in computer science. The reason is that improving the HCI so that humans can feel more at ease when working with computers, commit fewer errors, and have less frustration, enhances productivity and enables computers to be more useful and more acceptable to wider groups of people, including those without advanced education.

User Interfaces

The early programmers and data entry operators used the keyboard as their primary means of data entry. The data was entered onto punched card and a stack of these was then read into computer storage by means of a card reader. The only output device from a computer was a printer. Note that this user interface was not interactive, or in in real-time.

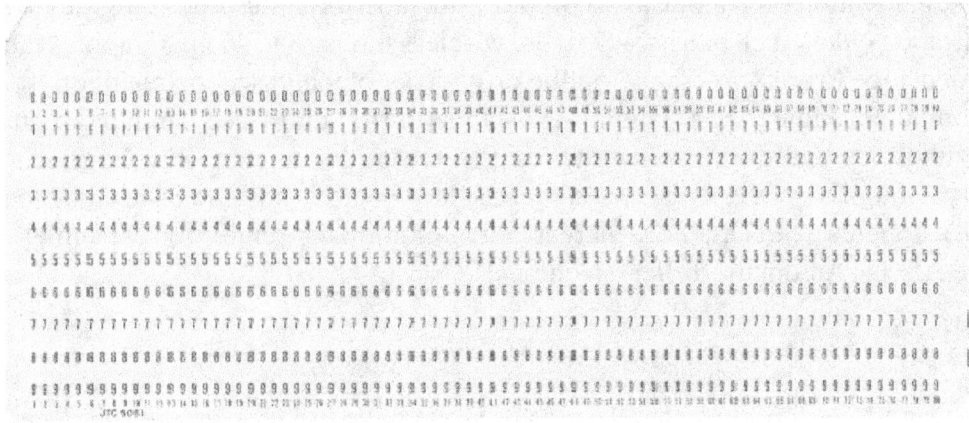

An early punch card.

In the 1980s these became replaced by terminals with screens (amber or green) and users entered information via a command-line interface. This interface allowed information to be entered only on specific lines and columns using whole characters (letters, numbers, symbols). No line graphics were possible.

HCI research at SRI International (Menlo Park, CA) and Xerox Palo Alto Research Center then led to the modern graphical user interface in which the screen is bit-mapped, enabling lines to be drawn on a screen that was soon capable of displaying first 64, then 256, then many hundreds and thousands of colors. On the hardware side, this led to the development of special video cards attached to the computer's motherboard whose only function is to draw on the screen. These video cards are computers in their own right, having specialized processors and memory. Roughly speaking they take the graphics as input (in digital form) provided by application software executing in real time and convert these into commands that can be understood by the computer's display. Computer displays have themselves become more sophisticated, with much finer screen resolutions (measured in dots per inch), larger sizes, the ability to display millions of colors, have higher refresh rates and so on. Most displays are now based on various flat panel technologies like liquid crystal (LCD) or light emitting diode (LED), unlike the bulky cathode ray tubes previously common. In addition to visual outputs, voice command and voice output have also become increasingly common.

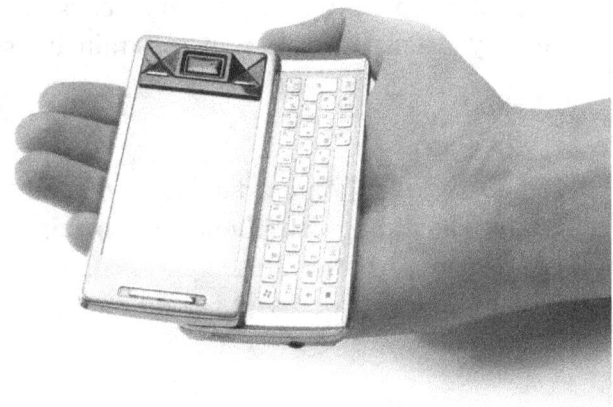

A modern PDA.

Hardware innovations for input to a computer include the mouse pointing device and its many variations like touch pads, track balls, wireless mouse and so on. Graphics tablets use a pen-like device to draw free-hand on the provided tablet and see the result on the screen. Tablet computers and Personal Digital Assistants (PDAs) allow users to tap directly on the screen with a pen and even use handwriting to create documents.(For large amounts of data entry, though, it is widely believed that the key-board is still the fastest data entry tool available). Touch screens are now increasingly common especially for consumer applications like ATMs (Automatic Teller Machines).

Software

Perhaps even more important than hardware is the software aspect, i.e., the design of the screens and data entry elements and organization of information on a screen. All of us have had the experience of using software (especially web sites) that are too busy, cluttered, have very un-intuitive logic, require you to enter the same data multiple times and so on.

User-interface designers now emphasize the use of scientific testing of user interfaces using design principles and testing on focus groups. One important consideration is the nature of the intended audience. For example, highly trained professionals like physicians will rapidly become impatient with simplistic or verbose presentations of medical information. However, inexperienced users may need precisely that kind of presentation. In other words, it is important to understand the mental model of the intended user with respect to the type of information presented. It is also important that the sequence (in which the computer asks for information while performing a task like making an airline reservation, for example) confirms how the intended audience typically performs that task. At the same time, it should use the power of the computer to actually make this experience more productive and faster than doing it manually. For example, automatic spell checkers, automatic pagination, embedded thesaurus and similar features can enable you to create professional documents easily and quickly.

Significance

Without the scientific discipline of HCI, computers would likely have remained only a tool for specialists. Enormous advances in the HW and SW aspects of HCI have enabled computers to be an every day tool of everyone in a modern society. While this has greatly benefited people, the increased use of computing has also caused some less desirable side effects such as carpal-tunnel syndrome, eyestrain, back strain and so on.

Impact on Future Technologies

The role of HCI will become increasingly important as computers become more and more ubiquitous. Mobile computing, including cell phones, are becoming a focus of this discipline. Robotics is another important frontier. Research in cognitive science (the discipline concerned with understanding thought processes) is being increasingly applied to HCI.

Concept Reinforcement:

1. Identify three web sites or software that, in your opinion, are poorly designed and explain why.

2. Identify three web sites or software that, in your opinion, are well designed and explain why.

3. Explain , giving examples, how and why user interface elements such as bright, flashing colors and loud noises can be appropriate in one application but inappropriate in another.

Section 2.15 – Social Implications of Information Processing

Section Objective:

- Understand the significance of the social implications of information processing on the science of computing, and analyze its impact on future technologies

What are the social implications of information processing?

The term *social implications of information processing* (SIIP) refers to the impact that information processing, especially by machines, has on people.

Clearly computing has had an enormous effect on society and on the lives of people. Some believe that not since the industrial revolution has any technology affected people in so many ways. Some of these effects have been beneficial and others have had unpleasant consequences.

Significance

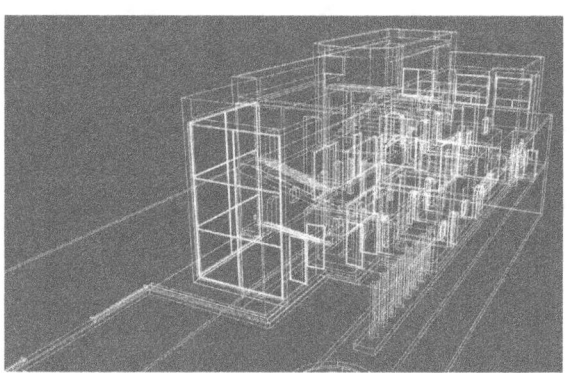

A CAD rendering of a house.

On the plus side, computing technology has been a great economic benefit, providing employment to possibly hundreds of millions of people worldwide if we count both he people directly involved in hardware manufacturing and software development and also those that gain indirectly from industries that have benefited from the use of information processing. For example, better aircraft have been designed and built using computing in all aspects from fluid mechanics to engineering design using CAD tools.

Computing, especially through the world wide web, has made it possible for anyone with an internet connection to contribute to knowledge resources and help others with their expertise. Similarly, there has never been so much information, on every conceivable topic, available so easily and cheaply. The number of entries in the free Wikipedia dwarfs in comparison to the rather expensive Encyclopedia Britannica. In the medical field, the ability of the computer to process large amounts of information very quickly has led to computer aided tomography (CAT) scanning and also makes MRIs possible. Using these physicians can vastly improve the accuracy of many kinds of diagnoses such as tumor detection.

Such beneficial consequences of computing have encouraged computer scientists and engineers to devise sophisticated and powerful systems to assist the solution of even more difficult problems, such as drug discovery and medical informatics. In practically every area of human endeavor, computing is being increasingly applied in productive ways. These new demands have led to advances in computer science and technology as well as the nature of information. Cognitive science is increasingly becoming important in this process.

However, information processing has also been the cause of harm in some ways. While information and knowledge posted on the web can often be trusted, coming from reputable individuals, there is also much misinformation, either from malice or from ignorance. Some use the anonymity of the internet to pass themselves off as experts on law, finance, medicine or whatever; the information they provide cannot be trusted, but it is not easy for lay persons to ascertain this. Our email boxes are the target of spammers and some have fallen victim believing somehow that the emailed offer to share in some ill-gotten millions is genuine.

The storage of ones personal information, including medical and psychological records, by entities out of one's control has led to the loss of privacy. The web is rife with offers to learn almost anything about anyone for a few dollars. Employers routinely search the web, including social networking sites, for any and all information about job seekers. Since image processing is so cheap, celebrities, (and ordinary persons), have had their likenesses copied into unsavory situations, and the results broadcast on the web. Some have been the target of malicious attacks in the form of false and compromising information (including images) placed in multiple locations. Last year, in the state of Missouri, a teenager committed suicide after becoming the victim of a prank played on her in the form of a fictitious male friend on a social networking site, who first befriended her and then turned upon her. Many individuals have been subject to identity theft. The social significance of these widely publicized incidents is to cause a mistrust of computing technologies.

Impact on Future Technologies

Some of these abuses could have technological solutions. Spam filters can help cut down the volume of unwanted junk mail. This necessitates research in developing criteria for identifying desirable versus undesirable messages. Research is also proceeding on improving security. There are companies that for a fee will scour the web for references about you and try to enforce the removal of damaging information.

A PDA/cell phone hybrid.

Information processing does not live in a vacuum. It is meant to serve the needs of people and will continue to do so in new and exciting forms. For many people in advanced countries, computers, the web, and other information processing technologies are as fundamental as water and food. Cell phones, which are an exciting mix of information and communication technology (ICT), will continue to make information processing even more pervasive.

Concept Reinforcement:

1. Identify three specific ways, not mentioned in the lesson, in which information processing has had a positive impact on people.

2. Identify three specific ways, not mentioned in the lesson, in which information processing has had a negative impact on people.

3. Identify some possible ways in which cell phones could impact society in the future.

Unit Three

Section 3.1 – Future Algorithms

Section Objective:

- Analyze how future algorithms may impact the science of computing

What are some trends in Algorithms research and development?

Advances in computing hardware technologies, data communications, cheap storage and sensors, including imaging, are proceeding at a rapid rate. These great strides also present interesting challenges in the development of software to take advantage of the availability of all this information. Since algorithms underlie of all software, including both systems and application software, much of the challenge falls on algorithms. To appreciate the nature of the challenge, one must first understand the notion of algorithm complexity.

In the broadest sense, the complexity of an algorithm relates to the amount of resources needed to execute the software. There are two kinds of algorithm complexity: space complexity and time complexity. The former is the amount of memory needed to run the algorithm and the second is the amount of time needed. For various reasons, including the cheap availability of vast amounts of storage, computer scientists are more concerned about time complexity. Hence in the following we shall concentrate on time complexity, and call it simply algorithm complexity.

Algorithm Complexity

An algorithm is a step by step procedure that is guaranteed to terminate. Most algorithms operate on input data. An algorithm for finding the square root of a number expects one number as input. A basic algorithm for multiplication expects two numbers as input. A fundamental notion in complexity analysis is the number of input data points, and is denoted N. Complexity theory also regards arithmetical operations like addition, subtraction, multiplication and division, and comparison, as the most basic operations performed by a computer. Therefore, the complexity of an algorithm is concerned with the rate of increase of the number of such operations, with respect to N. For example, a simple algorithm to multiply a list of N numbers will first multiply the first two, then multiply with the result with the 3rd, and continue until the last number in the list. In other words, N multiplications have to be performed.

Now consider sorting N numbers using the following comparison sort algorithm.

- Start: Count the size of the list. Denote by N.

- Compare the first element of the list of N elements against all the others and discover the smallest. Set it aside in the first location in a *destination list*. (Note that there are now N-1 numbers in the remaining unsorted list)

- Now repeat step number 2 for the *remaining* unsorted list until the remaining list is empty. At each execution of step 2, the smallest number found is assigned a place *after* the existing ones in the destination list.

Stopping rule: Terminate the algorithm when the remaining list is empty

This algorithm requires the computer to perform approximately N^2 comparisons. Since different computers have different CPUs, it is possible that the real time will be 0.001 N^2 seconds on one and 0.5 N^2 seconds on another. However, you cannot get rid of the N^2 factor. Computer scientists say that the comparison sort algorithm described above has time complexity of the order of N^2, written as $O(N^2)$. Similarly, there are problems and algorithms whose complexities are in the order of higher powers of N. These are called polynomial time algorithms. The $O()$ notation is a measure of the speed of an algorithm. An $O(N^2)$.algorithm is faster than an $O(N^{10})$ algorithm because the rate of growth of the former, with respect to N, is less than the rate of growth of the latter.

Now consider this apparently simple problem called the Traveling Salesman Problem: A salesman needs to visit N cities and return home. Find the path that minimizes the cost of the entire trip.

It turns out that the fastest known algorithm for this problem has complexity $O(2^N N^2)$.

It is the exponential, 2^N term, that is the killer here because it increases much faster with respect to N, than the square of N. In fact, when N = 10, the number of computations is 102,400 and merely doubling N results in the need for 419,430,400 computations.

The traveling salesman problem is not unique in this sense. It is only one of a very large collection of problems in various fields that has exponential complexity.

So, a big challenge in the future will be devising solutions to exponentially complex problems that may not yield exact solutions but could yield approximate solutions quickly.

Some computer scientists have proposed Genetic Algorithms for this purpose. A genetic algorithm generates many possible solutions to a problem then applies a fitness function to select the best among them. The process is continued until only one (or very few) solutions remain.

Concept Reinforcement:

1. Identify three trends in computing leading to the need to process vast amounts of data (vast means more than 100 Giga Bytes)

2. Which is faster: An $O(2^N)$ algorithm or an $O(N^2)$ algorithm?

3. Describe the purpose of a generic algorithm.

Section 3.2 – Future Languages

Section Objective:

- Analyze how future computer languages may impact the science of computing

What are some trends in computer languages?

Some general-purpose languages commonly in use today are JAVA, Visual C++, Visual BASIC, PERL, C. The first three support the paradigm of *object-orientation*.

Over the years, computer scientists and researchers have identified other paradigms that can be useful in programming. Some of these are the following.

Dynamism: The language can add new code or data types while it is running and thereby extend itself. The AI language LISP was one of the first to have this capability. PYTHON and MAUDE are two languages that support this today.

Reflection: The language has the capability to observe its own execution and modify its behavior. JAVA and C++ support some types of reflection. One example of reflection in action is when a program uses a string of letters (possibly generated during program execution) as a variable name or, if syntactically correct, as program code.

Imperative Programming: Here, the statements of the language are commands to perform specific actions that the program should perform. FORTRAN and JAVA are imperative languages. This is in contrast to *declarative* programming in which the program describes what an entity is like. An example is HTML (Hypertext markup language) used to describe web pages.

RUBY

A general purpose programming language that is increasingly popular is an interpreted language called RUBY. Interpreted means that program statements are converted into machine language and executed in real time, for example, as soon as the programmer hits the 'Enter' key. This is in contrast to *compiled* languages (like JAVA) that require submission of a complete program to the compiler first and creation of an executable. Apart from being object-oriented, RUBY supports multiple paradigms including those listed above. Originating from Japan, RUBY has achieved popularity because its syntax is elegant, looks clean and thereby supports simplicity.

AJAX

A collection of techniques that is becoming popular for web programming is AJAX (Asynchronous JavaScript and XML). JavaScript is a scripting language that can be embedded within web pages and executed within a web browser (like Internet Explorer). XML (Extended Markup Language) is a specification to create markup languages (like HTML) and that can also be used to describe complex structured data. XML can serve as a data interchange system. Multiple programs can read the same XML data content, extract information relevant their needs and process accordingly. The asynchronous part refers to retrieving or writing data from external sources while the web page is being displayed.

Summary

Languages are often developed to serve specific needs that arise in computation. The need to share data and applications over the web led to the creation of several new languages like HTML, JavaScript, ASP, PHP, and others. As computing changes in the future, new languages will be developed to meet new requirements. Mobile computing (cell phones, PDAs) and robotics are future computing environments that may drive the creation of new languages or improvements of old ones.

Concept Reinforcement:

1. Is there a programming language that you use regularly? What improvements would you like to add to it?

2. What kind of special functionality so you think will be needed in a language designed to program a mobile robot that performs household chores?

3. Explain further the difference between interpreted and compiled languages.

Section 3.3 – Future Computer Design

Section Objective:

- Analyze how future developments in computer design may impact the science of computing

What are some trends in computer design?

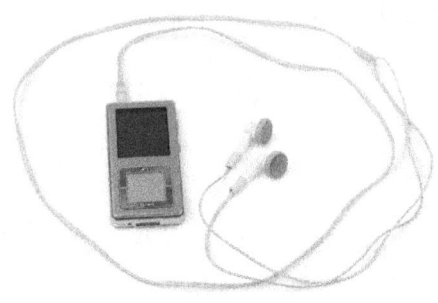

A pink mp3 player.

Over the last 50 years computing has seen an incredible amount of progress and innovation. The supercomputer of 15 years ago, which occupied a room and needed large quantities of electricity and air-conditioning, is the laptop of today. Peripherals like printers, scanners, wireless networking, digital cameras, cell-phones and computing-based gadgets like MP3/MPEG players have undergone miniaturization, available in very attractive colors and designs. Putting it another way, computers and compute-intensive devices are now becoming consumer devices, rather than programmers.

For this reason, especially for desktop and laptop computers, product design is playing an increasingly important role. This refers to the shape, form-factor, appearance, weight, and colors of the device. Laptop manufacturers find that consumers are willing to pay a premium price for lighter and thinner laptops. This raises interesting issues for computer scientists and engineers who are asked to pack more bytes into smaller volumes for secondary disk storage, produce brighter screens, engineer faster processors that consume less power, and also develop batteries that are lighter and last longer. Software engineers are tasked with developing intelligent power management systems and user friendly software that includes gesture recognition, voice input, voice output (including human-sounding text-to-speech), handwriting recognition, word/command completion and many other innovations.

Progress is demonstrably being made in all these areas. Recently the multi-touch user interface has been developed. This is an extension of the familiar touch screen in which, instead of just one finger touching the screen and acting as a mouse button, multiple fingers touch the screen and the computer responds in an intuitively appropriate manner. In addition, flexible displays, which can be rolled up like a newspaper, are rapidly nearing commercialization. One such, albeit with a small form factor, was recently announced.

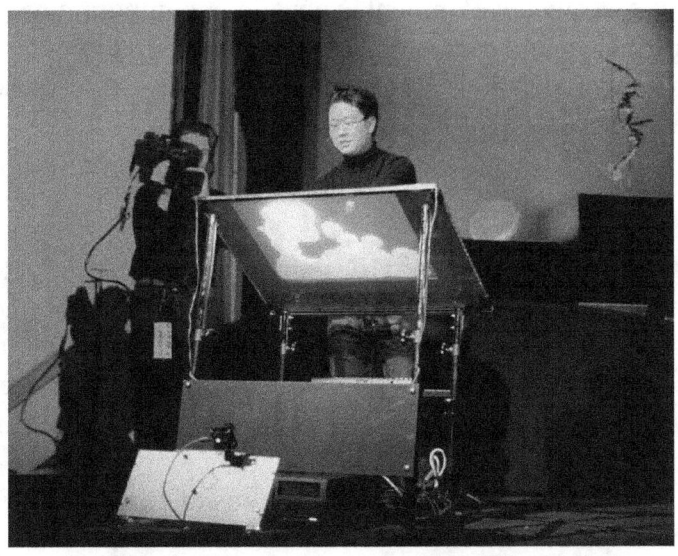

A multi-touch screen courtesy of Jurvetson.

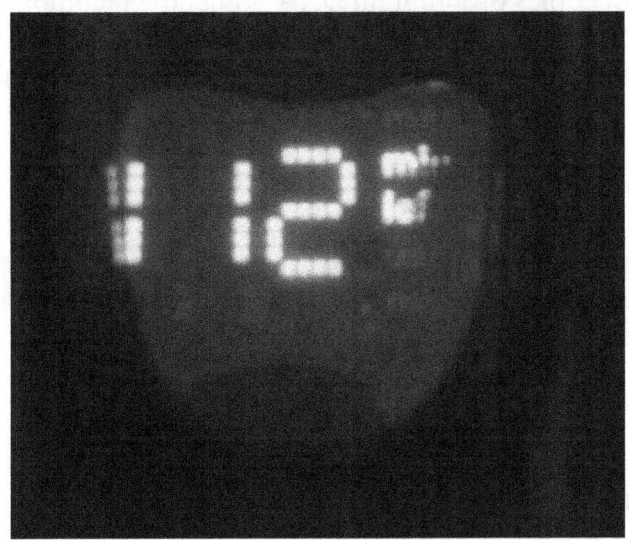

A close-up of a flexible display on an electric razor.

Heads-up displays can be built into eyeglasses or attached to them. These are connected to a computers output and replace the standard monitor. Since the heads-up display is so close to the eye it gives the appearance of a large screen in a small and light form factor. Some heads up displays are see-through, in the sense that, by shifting focus, the user can have either normal vision or look at the computer display. Heads-up displays that project onto an aircraft's windshield are features in some military aircraft.

These can also support developing augmented reality in which live images and sounds are enhanced by computer generated ones.

The trend towards miniaturization and smaller screens, as in PDAs and mobile phones raises interesting issues for screen designs. Are there innovative ways in which small screens can provide large amounts of information? What kinds of user-input technologies can be devised to augment the now-familiar thumb keyboards or soft-keyboards (as in the iPhones)?

For a time, another interesting development in consumer computing was the wearable computer in which the processor and other components are integrated into clothing or attached to the wrist. Currently there has been some interest in integrating sensors that track body vital signs into a wearable format.

Biological computing

Some researchers are very intrigued with designing and developing so-called biological computers. These are devices that use biological objects to perform computations. DNA computing is one such idea. This is inspired by the observation that the DNA sequence encodes information in a digital format and strands of DNA can be several billion digits long while occupying exceedingly tiny volumes. Theoretically, therefore, we can encode any digital string, including a complete program and data, into strands of DNA. DNA can also be replicated with very high accuracy into millions of copies. So, if we could encode a program into a DNA sequence, replicate it millions of times, and at the same time encode the data on which the program is to operate into other strands of DNA then we may be able to make the millions of copies of 'program DNA' somehow recombine with the millions of 'data DNA' and read off the answers in the output DNA sequences. One further benefit of this process, if it can be reliably implemented, is that very little energy is required and no heat is produced.

Summary

In both the consumer and research areas, the desire and need to push the frontiers of computer design continue to pose new and interesting challenges to computer scientists, software engineers and technologists.

Concept Reinforcement:

1. What new design challenges arise from wearable computers?

2. What are the user-interface challenges, for both input and output, on small form-factor computers, like cell phones?

3. Describe some of the features demanded by consumers in new computer products.

Section 3.4 – Future Databases

Section Objective:

- Analyze how future databases may impact the science of computing

What are some trends in database research and development?

Database technology, i.e., the ability to easily store, edit, process, organize, retrieve, and ask simple to complex questions of stored information has been integral to the success of computing. The relational data base model of information has dominated database technology. This model is well suited to certain kinds of data such as employee records, sales transactions and similar and has shown itself to be remarkably adaptable to store complex data. .

However, for certain kinds of information, other database models have been suggested. One of these is the object-oriented database (OOD). The need for OOD arose because commonly used programming languages are object-oriented and within these, data is represented as objects. It would be very convenient if the same representation were to be used in the database as in the programming language. However, most database systems in use are relational. Several attempts have been made in the last decade to develop and popularize OODs, but relational databases still dominate. However, a hybrid called an object relational database system (ORD) is now gaining in popularity.

A historic cat scan machine.

Another trend is the increasing use of image databases, fueled in large part by the popularity of digital cameras. Quite apart from storing family vacation pictures in an organized way, image databases have more serious applications, such as repositories of X-Rays, CAT scans, MRIs, and similar medical images. Some challenges for image databases is that they are very large, especially at the resolution needed for medical purpose, and a single MRI could easily produce hundreds of Megabytes of storage. An interesting software challenge is how to search images databases in a pictorial, rather than textual way. For example, a researcher in orthopedics may want to find all pictures showing a hairline fracture of thigh bones.

Closely related to image databases is audio storage. Similar challenges arise. And all of these come together when we start considering databases of videos. Naturally, a current solution for the query problem is to tag the multi-media content with textual keywords, and perform searches on these keywords. However, it is clear that there is loss of information since no tags can adequately capture the richness of images, audio, or video.

The ability to collect large amounts of data in turn leads to the need to store these. Think, for example, of the amount of data that is generated on patients in a hospital. Quite apart from images, vast quantities of medical information such as continuous monitoring of vital signs, lab tests, physicians notes, and measurements of blood chemicals are generated.

This has led to an active area of research called *Very Large Databases*. These researchers seek ways to efficiently and quickly provide all the database functionality that we have grown to expect.

These are some of the challenges being faced by database researchers today.

Concept Reinforcement:

1. Describe some trends in database development.

2. Explain an object-oriented database.

3. Discuss the relationship between generating large files, such as image and audio files, and storage of those files.

Section 3.5 – Future Processors

Section Objective:

- Analyze how future processors may impact the science of computing

What are the some trends in processor research and development?

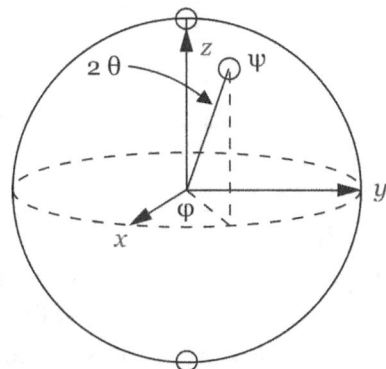

A blochsphere, a building block of a quantum computer.

While processors have made phenomenal improvements in the last 50 years mankind's appetite for computing has correspondingly increased. Some computer science researchers have focused on the limitations imposed by the fact that processors (and memory) are still based on binary logic. The circuits implementing binary logic can exist in one of only two states, represented conventionally as a 0 or a 1. All data, and all program instructions exist within the computer, and in memory storage as strings of 0s and 1s taken eight at a time. Eight bits are, of course, a *byte*. Since a byte corresponds to one letter or digit, to represent 1000 letters or strings in a computer needs 8000 bits.

An area of great interest among some computer scientists and engineers today is *Quantum computing*, and the use of a *qubit* as the basic unit of information storage. A qubit is an entity that can assume the values 0 and 1 but also anything in between. So, in theory, a single qubit can represent any string, no matter how long it is. Also, it has been shown, in theory that a quantum computer (QC) would be capable of solving very rapidly some problems that conventional computers can take years to solve. One of these is to factorize large numbers. Since the difficulty of this factorization is the basis of today's encryption algorithms quantum computing is of great interest.

However, many difficulties exist in developing QCs in the lab, let alone getting to the point of buying a QC at the local computer store. One difficulty is that the qubits developed so far have a tendency to lose state, i.e., the value they are storing. This is called *decoherence*. Another difficulty is developing hardware architectures underlying quantum computers. In spite of these problems, the potential benefits continue to motivate computer scientists performing QC research.

An exciting invention that was announced in early 2008 is called a *memristor*. Although the existence of this had been mathematically predicted in 1971 no one had succeeded in building one until a team from HP Labs, in Palo Alto, California did so using *nanotechnology*. A memristor is an electronic component with two terminals. Its electrical resistance depends on the current flowing through it. If the current flows in one direction the resistance increases and if it flows in the opposite direction the resistance decreases. If the current stops flowing and then is restarted the device maintains the resistance it had when the current was switched off. This property is called *memristance*.

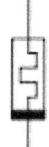

The symbol for a memristor, courtesy of MovGPO.

Memristors have remarkable properties with very significant implications for computing. Since they maintain the same resistance value so long as the current remains the same, and this can be varied simply by changing the current flow, a memristor can theoretically store multiple values, not just the 0 or 1 that current binary logic devices can. Thus, it is theoretically possible to achieve great data compression.

Further, since memristors remember the resistance they last had, even after they have been switched off, one can construct long lasting memory based not on semiconductor circuits as in Flash, or magnetic or optical properties. (Flash, also known as *semiconductor memory*, is the technology used in thumb drives) What is more, memristors have the potential to be much faster than Flash. This means that they could be the basis for computers, (not just small PDAs) that when power is switched on, return to the same state as when they were last switched off, displaying the last desktop and continuing any ongoing computations.

Summary

Research in advanced processors continues on many fronts, including developing multi-core CPUs (those with more than one processor on a single chip). Quantum computing and memristors are two exciting future technologies.

Concept Reinforcement:

1. What are the implications for data communications of being able to store a range of values, not just 0 or 1, in an electronic component?

2. What are the implications for computing of being able to store a range of values, not just 0 or 1, in an electronic component?

Section 3.6 – Future Artificial Intelligence

Section Objective:

- Analyze how future developments in Artificial Intelligence (AI) may impact the science of computing

What are some trends in Artificial Intelligence research and development?

Many researchers in Artificial Intelligence (AI) define two kinds of AI: *Strong AI* attempts to duplicate all of human intelligence, while *Narrow AI* is concerned with automated performance of specific tasks that are associated with intelligence

Narrow Artificial Intelligence

Honda's ASIMOV robot.

In recent years, much progress has been made on quite a few of the problems associated with narrow AI. Even if the AI label is not explicitly being applied to them, these areas can be associated with genuine intelligence and cognition. The distinction between AI and just plain computing can sometimes be hard to define. For example, spell checking is commonly concerned to be simple computing, while grammar checking is often considered to be (narrow) AI.

Some problems addressed by narrow AI, include voice recognition (VR), text-to-speech, machine vision, gesture recognition, and robotics, among others. VR is being almost routinely used by many companies, including airlines, when you call their phone numbers. Gesture recognition is used in Apple's iPhone. Machine vision has steadily made progress, being used in industrial applications. Robots that can vacuum floors, navigating around obstacles and the physical layout of walls and furniture, are commercially available. Robotics is one field that seems to bring all these technologies together, even to the extent of evoking emotional reactions among humans towards the robots. Sony's robotic dogs were an example. Recently, humanoid robots that can walk, dance, and respond to human-robot interactions have been developed by Honda.

The AI techniques underlying these innovations include the encoding of *heuristics*, i.e., "thumb rules," and common-sense reasoning. *Neural networks* are software analogs of the network of neurons comprising human (and animal) brains. These can learn to recognize patterns in data. *Machine learning* also plays a great role. This is concerned with algorithms and techniques that enable computers to gather knowledge, typically in a narrow domain, and use that knowledge to solve problems in that domain. Apart from the applications mentioned in the above, machine learning has been used in software that detects fraud, control of automobiles, games, and others. ML techniques are often based on statistics, and utilize *fuzzy logic,* in which we don't classify a statement into just two states: True or False, but also allow for some uncertainty in between. Agent-based systems consist of more-or-less autonomous software objects that can sense their environment and communicate with others. These are sometimes called *bots* and have been applied in several areas such as helping internet shoppers find items similar to what they were searching for, identifying potential faults in computer networks and others.

Strong Artificial Intelligence

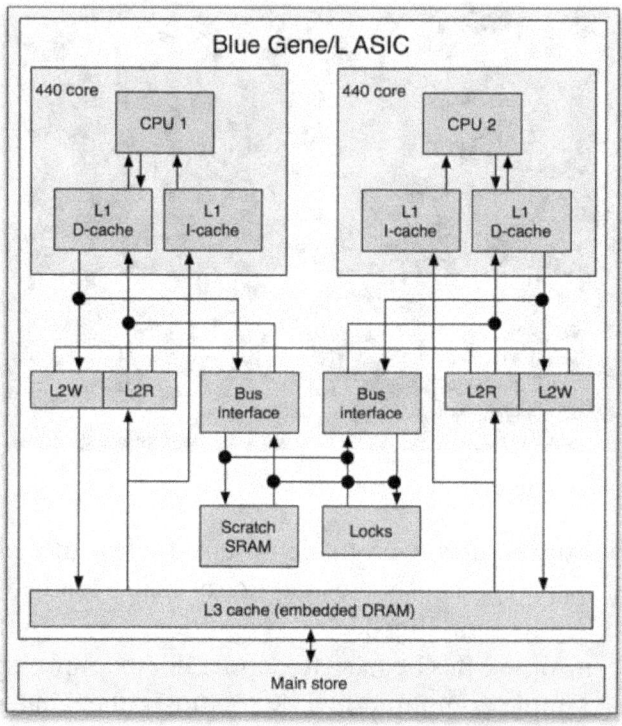

The block scheme for BlueGene.

Human intelligence has numerous attributes and features including consciousness, emotions, situational awareness, perception, interactions with other humans, personality, emotional intelligence, creativity in the arts, ability to make discoveries in the sciences, and many others. Can a machine be programmed to display at least a substantial subset of these? This is the question asked by researchers in Strong AI, also known as Artificial General Intelligence (AGI). An interesting question to ask is how powerful the hardware of a computer must be to achieve AGI. Estimates are in the range of 10^{13} instructions per second. Some special purpose computers such as IBM's BlueGene approach this kind of performance.

An even more interesting question is the design of the software needed to achieve AGI. Clearly, this will need much more research in cognitive science, i.e., the study of mind. Some computer scientists believe that thought processing by humans does not follow standard computational rules. Rather, a special architecture of cognition is needed.

Alan Turing, the father of computer science, also pondered the question of whether a machine could replicate human intelligence. To answer this question he proposed the famous Turing Test. Here, a human (H) interacts via a display and keyboard with another entity (E). The human, H, does not know if the other entity is a human or a computer. H uses the keyboard to engage in a question/answer conversation with E, using natural language, such as English. If, after a period of time, H cannot tell whether E is a human or a computer, then E is said to have passed the test and can be deemed to have human intelligence. To date, no computer seems to have passed the Turing test.

Other computer scientists have proposed another test of AGI. If a computer can tell situation-appropriate jokes, and laugh in response to a joke, then it would have achieved human intelligence.

Concept Reinforcement:

1. Explain the distinction between narrow AI and AGI.

2. What is the goal of machine learning?

3. Do you think grammar checking a document should be considered 'ordinary' computing, or AI? Explain why or why not.

Section 3.7 – Future Operating Systems

Section Objective:

- Analyze how future developments in Operating Systems may impact the science of computing

What are some trends in Operating Systems research and development?

Corresponding to the ever-increasing applications of computing and the various forms of computers themselves is enormous growth of research and development in the area of operating systems (OS).

For server computers, such as those running web sites, and databases, LINUX and Windows Server are the most common operating systems.

In the personal computer desktop area MacOS and Windows continue to become more sophisticated, providing more support for security, multi-tasking, and, soon to come, support for multi-core processors. Some versions of Windows VISTA (depending on the graphics card installed) provide a 3-D user interface. As processors and graphics hardware become more powerful, 3-D UIs may become even more common.

Mobile computing, in the form of Personal Digital Assistants, smart phones, wearable computers is an exciting trend in computing. Smart phones combine voice communications over the cellular network with data communications, internet access, and many features of general purpose computing. Operating systems for mobile computing need to support multi-tasking, provide fast switching between applications, and also support the real-time handling of incoming and outgoing voice communications. The SYMBIAN operating system supported by JAVA programming is an example of such an OS.

A close-up of a cell phone.

Windows is also steadily providing greater support for mobile computing in the form of Windows Mobile, a version of Windows designed specifically for mobile computing including PDAs and cell phones. One benefit of Windows Mobile is its compatibility with (desktop) Windows in terms of data sharing and synchronization. In addition, many Windows applications like Word, Excel, Windows Media Player, and SqlServer (Database management system) also execute in a limited form on mobile devices. The IOS operating system underlies Apple Computer's iPhones, iPod Touch's, and iPads. The Android operating system from Google is also a major OS for mobile phones and tablets.

Operating Systems and the Web

Nowadays, access to the web is so pervasive that stand-alone computing is often seen as an anachronism. Thus, the separation between the web and the desktop (or laptop) is steadily decreasing. To save on licensing costs many businesses and individuals prefer to use web-based versions of common application software. Companies like IBM and Amazon offer compute capacity to users worldwide just as electric companies offer electricity to remote customers. Corresponding to this trend, Operating Systems also may be increasingly engineered to enhance seamlessness between the desktop and the web.

Real Time Operating Systems

A Real Time Operating System (RTOS) is designed to support computers specialized to functionality whose successful completion must occur according to time constraints. For example, a rocket guidance system needs to operate in real time because many tasks managed by the system, such as calculating course trajectories, firing the rocket engines and so on must occur at specific time points and within specific time limits in order to be successful. Other real time contexts include some kinds of games, industrial robots, medical instrumentation, mobile phones, and airline reservations systems.

RTOS's are frequently installed in embedded computers. These are computers that, unlike general purpose computers, are designed in terms of hardware architecture to perform specialized functions. Examples include network routers, and industrial process controllers. The role of embedded computing is steadily increasing as many industrial products including automobiles take increasing advantage of computing. For this reason, while RTOS's have been in existence for decades now, it is likely that they will play an increasingly greater role. Some examples of RTOSs are QNX, VxWorks, and Mobile LINUX.

A black network router.

Concept Reinforcement:

1. Explain the benefits of a 3-D user interfaces to a desktop (or laptop) OS.

2. Explain with examples, how real time computing differs from running the usual desktop (laptop) applications?

3. What is mobile computing?

Section 3.8 – Future Architectures

Section Objective:

- Analyze how future architectures may impact the science of computing

What are some trends in computer architecture research and development?

Since Computer architecture is so fundamental to the advancement of computing, research and development in this field occurs worldwide and many directions are being pursued. Many of these are oriented towards High performance computing (HPC), i.e., to develop more advanced supercomputers whose speeds are in the neighborhood of teraFLOPS. FLOPS are Floating point Operation per Second, for example multiplication involving numbers with decimals, as opposed to whole numbers. FLOPS is a generally accepted measure of computer performance especially in the scientific and technical fields. One TeraFLOPS corresponds to one trillion floating point operations per second, and one trillion = 1,000,000,000,000. Some supercomputers, like IBM's Roadrunner have achieved one PetaFLOPS. This is 10^{15} floating point operations per second. However, this machine evidently needed enormous efforts and expense to build and the goal is to get teraflop performance in a more sustainable way.

The underlying architectural model that is being pursued is parallel computing, an idea that has been around for a while and has benefited recently from development is processor and communications technologies. Here multiple processors connected to the same memory store simultaneously work on different portions of a computation simultaneously and the final results are pooled together. Some of these processors could be specialized for specific types of computing, like 3-D graphics. A related architecture is distributed computing, which again utilizes multiple processors but these do not share the same memory store. Instead, the processors communicate with each other by message passing over high speed data links, typically over a Local Area Network. Cluster computing is an example of such a distributed architecture. Performance improvement can also be achieved in both parallel and distributed computing by load sharing in which tasks are migrated from overloaded processors to under-loaded ones, leading to overall performance improvement.

It should not be imagined that parallel computing is a panacea for all computation problems. When there are data dependencies between portions of a program, these cannot be parallelized and are necessarily sequential. For example, the operations of removing a certain amount of money from your bank account, which necessitates comparison of the requested amount to your bank funds, and calculating the balance after giving you the amount must be done in that sequence and not simultaneously. Thus, the total amount of parallelization that can be possible in a particular problem is limited by the sequential portions if any. Also, writing parallel programs is harder than writing sequential ones because the multiple processes executing in parallel must be synchronized.

In spite of this limitation there is a large class of compute intensive problems that can benefit greatly from parallelization. Some of these are in the fields of fluid dynamics, computer graphics, and animation.

Current Efforts in Parallelization

Developing scalable parallel architectures is a formidably difficult task that requires top quality skills in computer science, engineering, mathematics, algorithms, and software development.

Two current directions for achieving parallel computing are based on multiple cores per processor, and on Field Programmable Gate Arrays. The former technology consists of embedding two or more processors within a single chip and several off the shelf computers already have dual chips like the Intel Pentium Z2180. However, to achieve the goals of HPC, it is anticipated that 100 to 1000 cores may be needed in a single chip. This raises considerable problems with respect to scalability and manufacturing. Hence, another approach being pursued in some research labs is based on FPGAs.

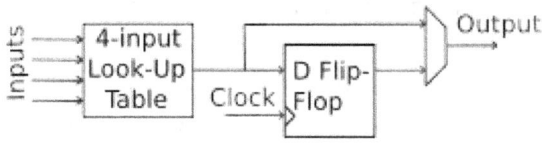

A diagram of a FPGA.

An FPGA consists of logic cells interconnected by wires and programmable switches. By means of special software in a Hardware Description Language (HDL) each of these logic cells can be given specific logic (AND, OR, NOR, etc) and the switches can be set so that the overall FPGA performs the desired functionality. Further, the program, and hence the functionality of the FPGA can be changed as often as needed.

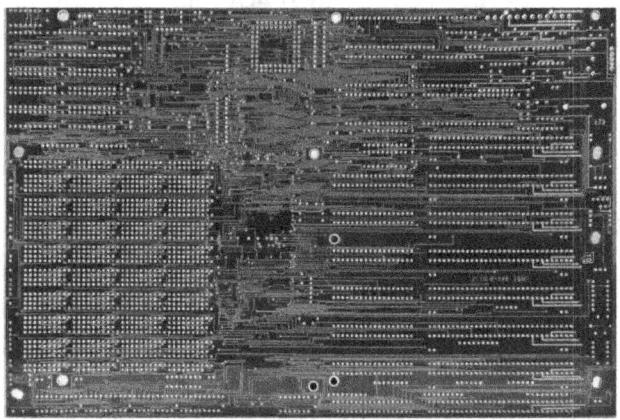

A generic circuit board.

In general FPGAs tend to be slower (often less than 500 Mhz) than CPUS and ASICs (Application Specific Integrated Circuits), and the programming is not easy. However, FPGAs have other advantages such as inherent capabilities for parallelism and much greater flexibility since the functionality of CPUs (like the Intel Pentium) or ASICs are set permanently at the lab. Therefore, many researchers are now using FPGAs as the basis for building scalable highly parallel high performance computers.

A challenge that is increasingly beginning to concern computer scientists is the memory wall. This is the name given to the fact that processor speeds are increasing much faster than memory speeds. Typically CPU speeds double every 18 months while memory speeds double every ten years. In other words, the rate of increase of memory speed is less than one fifth that of CPU speeds. Currently, for example, access from RAM can take up to 200 computer clock cycles while a floating point multiplication takes only 4 cycles. Broadly, speaking this means that the CPU can consume information faster than memory can supply it. Clever use of parallelism can help mitigate some of the effects of the memory wall. In addition, progress has been reported on a new kind of memory called Magnetic RAM (MRAM) that can potentially breach the memory wall.

Concept Reinforcement:

1. Give an example (not in the text above) of a computational problem that can be parallelized and explain why.

2. Give an example (not in the text above) that cannot be parallelized and explain why.

3. Explain why the memory wall can decrease computer performance.

Section 3.9 – Future Computer Graphics

Section Objective:

- Analyze how future developments in Computer Graphics may impact the science of computing

What are some trends in Computer Graphics research and development?

Progress in Computer Graphics (CG) includes advances in graphics hardware as well as software. Graphics hardware includes displays and also *graphics cards*. The function of the graphics card (also known as a video card) is to generate images for display. High-end graphics cards are attached to slots on the computer's motherboard and have analog and/or digital outputs (DVI). Many computers (including most laptops) integrate the graphics card onto the motherboard itself.

A modern GPU.

Graphics cards typically contain a specialized microprocessor called the *Graphics Processing Unit* (GPU). Unlike microprocessors for general purpose computing, such as the Pentium or the Turion, GPUs are designed to do complex floating point calculations very efficiently. A floating point calculation is one that involves numbers containing decimals. Such calculations are needed to light up *pixels* (picture elements) and thereby *render* images, i.e., produce the final full color image, with shadows, reflections, transparency, textures, and all the other image features that contribute to rich and realistic images. Further, to support high end animation, the video card must be capable of calculating entire new images up to 30 times/second. As displays steadily increase in size the graphics card has to produce high-quality rich images over larger screens. GPUs have built-in hardware circuitry to produce common shapes like lines, circles, triangles, squares and similar polygons. In addition, algorithms for 3-D rotations, transformations, shading, and similar can also be 'hard-wired' into the chip. Since such shapes and algorithms are the basic building blocks of more complicated 3-D shapes, GPUs can render complex images at high speed. Thus, an important focus of research in CG is the design of GPUs and associated circuitry. In fact, since one of the functions of a graphics card is to support animation, computer scientists are also developing Physics Processing Units (PPUs). These are processors that are customized to perform calculations associated with dynamics of various kinds including motion of fluids and of rigid bodies, light scattering, and fracture. Such PPUs can work in tandem with GPUs to produce realistic images and animations.

The GPU is located underneath the heatsink.

3-D displays

All the computer displays in common use these days are 2-dimensional displays. Using mathematical algorithms encoded in GPUs, 3-D realism can be obtained by appropriately lighting up and coloring pixels on the display. Some computer scientists and engineers are developing true 3-D displays in which the image occupies 3 full dimensions, not just two. The analog to pixel in such displays is the *voxel* (volume element) and such displays are called *volumetric* displays. Unlike 3-D movies, these displays can be viewed by the naked eye. One interesting technology for such displays is called *swept-surface,* and it usually involves rotating a surface around a central axis encased in a glass dome, and projecting images on to this surface. The images are computed in such a way that, aided by persistence of vision, the final image appears to be three dimensional. So far, the displays produced have been relatively small, about 10" in diameter.

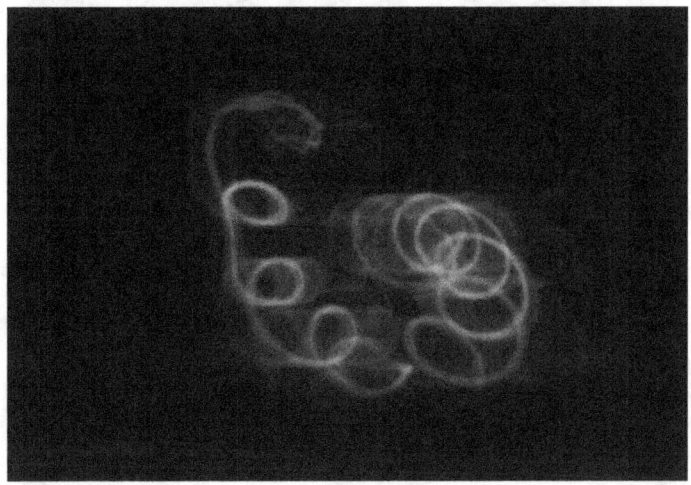

A volumetric image created by an actuality system courtesy of Holglyphics.

Such 3-D displays have been used for research in medical and physical simulations. Thus, they can aid in scientific visualization.

Software for computer graphics is usually based upon complex mathematics and associated algorithms to encode these into fast code. An important technique for producing images of stunning realism, including effects such as reflection, refraction, subtle color shades, transparency and translucency is *ray tracing*. The core idea of ray tracing is to follow the path of light rays from a light source until they hit an object, and then to calculate the value of the appropriate pixels based on the objects capacity for reflecting, absorbing, or scattering light at different colors. While ray tracing has been known since the 1960s as being one of the best methods to achieve photo realism, the techniques is computationally rather slow. So, one focus of research in CG is to develop faster and more powerful ray tracing algorithms. *Photon-mapping* is a promising approach in this direction. Here, the various effects on a light ray are computed simultaneously along its entire path, instead of sequentially. The technique allows very fast computation of images that involve a lot of light scattering such as headlights through a fog.

It can be expected that as such innovations move into the mainstream, commercial CG software systems will be updated to include these. A truly exciting phase in CG will occur when these exciting advances get applied to true 3-D (volumetric displays), and to large immersive environments (in which the viewer appears to be located within the image, not just looking in) thus moving far beyond 2-D displays.

A ray traced image.

Concept Reinforcement:

1. Explain the difference between a voxel and a pixel.

2. What are some potential applications for 3-D (volumetric) displays?

Section 3.10 – Future Computer Animation

Section Objective:

- Analyze how future developments in Computer Animation may impact the science of computing

What are some trends in Computer Animation research and development?

Computer Animation (CA) is playing an increasingly important role in the entertainment industry including movies and games. Taken together, these two industries represent tens of billions of dollars in yearly revenue. Madagascar, Shrek, The Incredibles, and other feature films are composed entirely in CA and many other movies use CA for special effects. The advertising industry also uses CA extensively in TV commercials.

With respect to the technology itself, *motion-capture* is emerging as an important method for capturing realistic motion. Here, humans wearing special sensors attached to various parts of their bodies perform physical activities in a motion-capture lab. The movements of the sensors in 3-D are recorded at high capture rates by optical equipment. These data can then be used to reconstruct the original movements in a computer. Once the motion has been captured the 3-D images of human or humanoid characters can be mapped onto the movements. It then appears that the humanoid character is performing the movements.

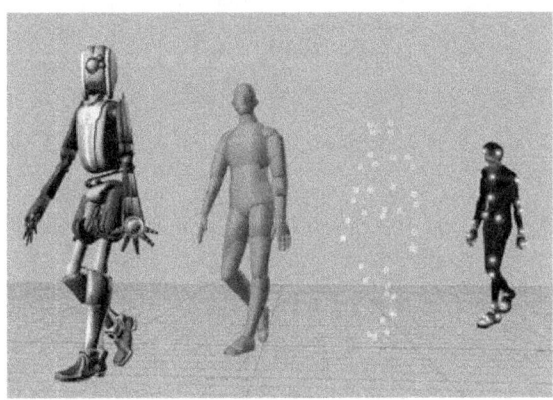

An image displaying motion capture being used to animate a character.

Because complicated movements such as dancing, acrobatics and similar are very difficult to generate algorithmically in a computer, motion-capture can save enormous time and effort and provide realistic motions to CA characters. However, even after the motion capture is completed, mapping a human figure onto the sensor trajectories is not trivial. One complicated task is *skinning*, in which the skin of the desired human must be overlaid on the computer animated figure being mapped onto motion capture data. This has to be done in such a way as to mimic the natural tightening, stretching, loosening, coloration, of skin that occurs during movements. Facial animation also has to cope with similar challenges.

Much of CA is based on complex mathematics and very sophisticated algorithms encoded in software. These can be very compute-intensive, especially when the final animation is created with up to 30 frames per second, in full color. This rendering process requires dozens of powerful computers networked together.

CA has also been explored for other applications, including medical simulations. Architects use CA techniques to produce realistic virtual walk-throughs of buildings they are designing. Flight simulators use CA extensively in pilot training. Here, 3-D physical motion of the simulator capsule is synchronized with CA and computer graphics to simulate aircraft movements. CA has also been used in *ride-films*. In ride films, people sit inside cars, as in roller coasters, and as the cars move along a track they are surrounded by 3-D computer animation. Immersive CA when combined with haptic equipment, that can simulate touching and pressure, can lead to 3-D virtual reality environments for training and entertainment.

Concept Reinforcement:

1. Apart from skinning what other aspects of humanoid figures must be mapped onto motion capture data to achieve realistic animation?

2. Design a ride-film of your own and describe the nature of the associated computer animation (images, movements, challenges).

Section 3.11 – Future Security

Section Objective:

- Analyze how future developments in Security may impact the science of computing

What are some trends in Security research and development?

It is an unfortunate fact of the digital life that our computers and, sometimes, we face security threats. The consequence of accidentally stumbling on a malicious web site, or unthinkingly opening an attachment in an email can be serious, resulting in a corrupted computer. This may require a complete erasure and reformat of the hard disk(s) causing at the very least, loss of time, effort, money, and productivity.

If one broadens the definition of security to include crimes committed using a computer and the web, then there have been incidents of people coming to physical harm due to interactions with people that they would not have met without the distance-bridging technologies provided by the internet. People who respond to the "Nigerian 419" scam letters, in which someone in a foreign country promises you a percentage of funds that you help transfer out of that country have lost substantial amounts of their money and, if they visit the foreign country, have been threatened with bodily harm.

Why are computers so vulnerable? There are several reasons. One is that the goal of enhancing usability and the goals of security can be in conflict. As an extreme example, a stand-alone computer in a locked room without any input data capabilities (except for a keyboard) in which the data is encrypted would be quite secure but also have poor access. Another reason is that software, especially operating systems software like Windows, Linux, is very complex, consisting of tens of millions of lines of code written by hundreds of programmers. Further, these OSs consist of tens of thousands of components. At any given time, a computer will be running anywhere from 25 to 50 individual processes (in Windows, click ctrl-alt-delete, to bring up Task manager and then click on the processes tab). It is almost impossible to check all of these for their potential security vulnerabilities. In addition, the programming languages C, in which huge amounts of software have been written is susceptible to buffer overflow problems in which the memory area allocated to a particular program variable could be exceeded during program execution if the programmer wasn't careful. In several cases, this buffer overflow in frequently used programs like mail or web browsers led to miscreants being able to gain control of the system being attacked.

Another source of security issues arises from the fact that the internet was designed with a lot of trust in mind, to enhance connectivity, access, and anonymity. Today, anyone, including criminals, can get into the internet from anywhere in the world under multiple false identities and be effectively invisible and unreachable, especially if they are located in countries that have poor law enforcement capabilities. Some governments also have been implicated.

Therefore, computer security faces lots of challenges and this is why it is foolhardy to connect a computer to the internet without first installing protection software that can detect the more common and well-known attacks. A particularly insidious attack attempts to gain administrator access to your computer and convert it into a bot. A bot is a puppet controlled by its owner and can be used in any manner the puppeteer chooses, most often for launching attacks on other computers and serving up unsavory and illegal content.

While security software can be very useful, note that it can protect only against attacks it already has prior knowledge about. This knowledge is called a signature. As soon as a new attack is reported, security software companies analyze it and encode the identifying characteristics into its unique signature. All customer copies of the software are then updated.

Another challenge is to measure exactly how vulnerable a particular system or software is. For example, Windows is usually regarded as more vulnerable than MacOS. But a quantitative score would be useful.

Spam, i.e., unwanted email is another challenging problem. It certainly is a problem: some estimate that 75% to 80% of all email sent out today is spam. This represents a huge waste of people, computing, and communications resources. Computer scientists are actively engaged in ways to identify spam and to develop spam filters. Unfortunately, some of these techniques can incorrectly tag desired email as spam.

To summarize, computer security is a growing problem. Recognizing this, many software vendors are now actively incorporating security features into their products. For example, the latest Windows software detects when a program is to be launched and asks the user if that is legitimate. This could protect users by warning them against potentially malicious executable software. Information Systems staff at large organizations have a very large responsibility to prevent data files like credit card numbers and medical records from being stolen or compromised. They also have to worry about Denial of Service attacks in which a web site is bombarded by hundreds of thousands of simultaneous requests causing it to crash. Such attacks can come from bots all over the world. There have been reports of blackmail attempts on businesses by criminals who threaten denial of service attacks unless they are paid off.

Concept Reinforcement:

1. What are some other kinds of attacks on computers not listed in the above?

2. What are some reasons for the vulnerability of computers not listed in the above?

3. Make a list of characteristics that identify spam emails. Apply them to a weeks worth of your email (you do not have to write the program, just apply your criteria). How many spam emails did your technique catch? How many of these were legitimate emails?

Section 3.12 – Future Software Engineering

Section Objective:

• Analyze how future developments in Software Engineering (SE) may impact the science of computing

What are some trends in Software Engineering?

Just a few decades ago when software development started becoming an important industry it was realized that the difficult task of writing industrial strength programs needed to develop methodologies and disciplines. One early such process was called the Waterfall model, which followed a sequence of developing requirements documents, functional specifications, design, implementation, verification, testing and then into a maintenance phase.

However, in many contexts this methodology has proved to be too rigid for modern needs. Experience has shown that it is almost impossible to define requirements in advance for software in all details, including the user interface. Instead, software engineers realized that a new methodology called *Agile Program Development* (AD) may be more beneficial to developers and customers alike. Actually, AP is more a philosophy or a collection of processes than a rigidly defined methodology.

Some features of AD include rapid development of system components, quick (in weeks) release to customers, *unit testing*, frequent consultation with the customer, refinement according to feedback, continuous changes in requirements as the customer sees the shape of the eventual product, simplicity, teams organized in small groups, and several others. Unit testing means that the software is tested module by module as soon as it is developed. An important benefit of AD is that the customer is kept very closely involved with the development progress, sees it evolving, can suggest changes and thus unpleasant surprises can be avoided.

To help manage agile development, a variety of tools have been developed. An example is *Scrum*. These tools include software (often web-based) for version tracking, reporting/tracking bugs and features, and team selection.

Extreme Programming

An interesting form of AP is called *Extreme Programming* (EP). Some features of EP include a loose form of user requirements called User stories, in which the customer (ideally the intended users of the projected system) write down their expectations of system components. These are used to assign tasks to developers who are then asked to estimate their own completion times for the tasks. Every day there is a progress review in a *stand-up meeting*. Such meetings tend to be quick and to-the-point. A hallmark of EP is *pair programming*. Here, two developers share a computer, pass the keyboard and mouse back and forth among themselves. While one is typing the other can look and point out any issues or think ahead to the next task. In many cases pair programming can lead to faster code development with fewer bugs.

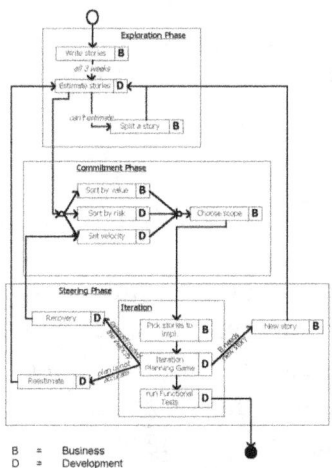

An example of extreme programming.

Cross-Platform development

It is clear that even on the near term, computing will occur not just on a desk-top or laptop PC but also as web applications and on mobile devices such as tablets and cell phones. Cross-platform development refers to developing software with the same functionality on all these platforms. Software development environments such as Microsoft's Visual Studio provide extensive support for developing software to run on Windows and Windows Mobile operating systems. A major challenge in cross-platform development is to account for varying screen sizes and screen navigation. To make sure the same program runs on small screens such as phones and large screen such as tablets, programmers typically get screen details from the operating system of the mobile device and adjust the screen elements of the program (app) accordingly.

Software engineering for robotics could also present some interesting challenges.

Concept Reinforcement:

1. What benefits do you see in pair programming? What are possible disadvantages?

2. Suppose you are writing a program that needs to run on multiple platforms, from cell phones to PDAs, to laptops and desktops. What are some challenges you may face?

Section 3.13 – Future Networking

Section Objective:

- Analyze how future developments in networking may impact the science of computing

What are some trends in networking research and development?

Currently it is rare to find a computer that is not linked to the internet or an internal company network (an intranet). The need for increasing speed of network access is steadily increasing, as more and more content, including full length movies, becomes available online. A similar need exists within company intranets as large multinational corporations strive to make the company's databases easily available to those employees needing access.

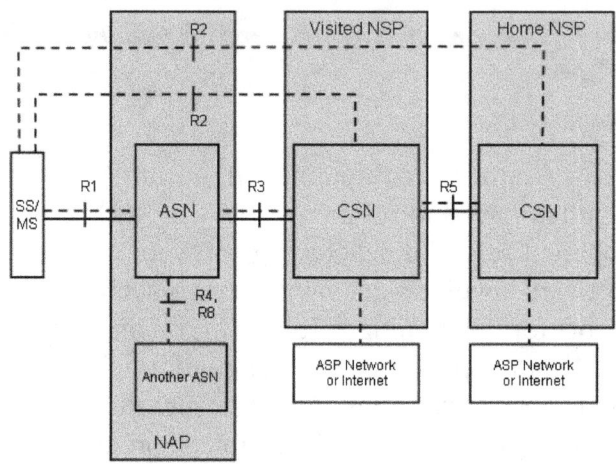

A diagram of the WiMAX architecture.

From a hardware point of view this means that computer scientists and engineers are continually developing new methods to enhance connectivity and network speed. Of course, fiber optic cable, Digital Subscriber Lines, Cable Modems, high speed wireless networks are some enabling technologies ion this regard, and networking companies are continually improving the speeds of these systems. In the wireless networking arena, an emerging trend is WiMax. Unlike conventional wi-fi networks that typically have limited range (100 to 150 yards), WiMax is designed to provide wireless networking across entire cities. To enhance database access within large corporations, a technology called SAN (Storage Area Networking) is now being deployed at company data centers. SAN includes encryption capabilities for data security.

In addition, networking is also becoming common in mobile phones, with many smartphones providing mobile internet access over the cellular network. Until quite recently email was the only reliable internet application available on some cell phones (like Blackberry). Nowadays many cell phones provide almost full featured web access especially where full 3G wireless service is available.

Many exciting developments are also occurring in the capabilities and future directions in the usage of the world wide web.

Web 2.0

A tag cloud illustrating Web 2.0 courtesy of Franzacurta.

The world-wide-web is a marvelous innovation, providing practically unlimited amounts of knowledge and functionality to anyone and anywhere. Web 2.0 is the name given to a rich collection of applications and standards that enhance the view of the web as being a platform for innovative applications enabling users to bridge distances and gain interactive access to worldwide resources, rather than just being a collection of data servers providing static data. Web 2.0 does not imply new hardware or technical specifications. (Of course faster web access and faster database access on the web-server side always enhance the web experience) Web conferencing, collaboration, social networking sites, multi-player games, alternate reality sites (like Second Life) and so on can be viewed as the Web 2.0 experience. Embedding of videos physically existing in one web site in other web sites is also an example. RSS (Real Simple Syndication) is a way to publish data from one web site to users on RSS feeder software that can either be on the web or on a desktop or perhaps a mobile smart phone.

All these are examples of Rich Internet Applications built using a complex of technologies include video/audio streaming, Adobe's Flash, and a common standard called XML (Extensible Markup Language) that extends the notion of HTML (Hypertext Markup Language). HTML specifies the way web pages are written and it is understood by all web browsers. In fact, XML is a standardized way to create custom markup languages (specialized HTMLs) and to describe data in a structured way.

XML can be regarded as a standard. i.e., a set of rules that are accepted worldwide. Because of this, software developers anywhere can write innovative programs that make use of XML standards for the exchange and broadcast of, for example, complex data.

RDF (Resource Description Framework) is another standard that enables software developers worldwide to describe internet-based resources such as web pages, As an extreme example, the contents of a web page could be described in the RDF standard.

As opposed to syntax, which describes the proper construction of sentences in a language, semantics is concerned with the meaning of the sentence. Currently, the basic unit of information on the web is a web page written in the mark-up language HTML. This consists of text, pictures, and of course controls like buttons and drop-down lists. However, even though current web pages have a meta-tag capability so that their authors can provide keywords to describe the page, there is really no way currently for web pages to give semantic descriptions of their contents, or place the contents in some wider knowledge framework. This is why we have to search the web using short words and phrases like "Rome" or "University Texas," instead of higher-level concepts like "Capital of Italy," or "Higher educational schools in Texas." Clearly, the semantic web would enable much more intuitive and human-like organization and searching of knowledge. The inventor of the web, Tim Berners-Lee and the Director of the W3C organization (The World Wide Web Consortium) is also one of the prime advocates of developing technologies to make the semantic web a reality.

To this end, computer scientists are actively developing standards and software. XML, RDF, OWL (Web Ontology Language) and others are being explored. An ontology can is a structured way to classify and organize knowledge concepts, and OWL is a family of languages for developing ontologies. A domain ontology refers to an ontology for a particular knowledge area such as medicine. These are important because the same word can mean different meanings depending on the domain. In a textbook of biology, 'web' would likely mean spider web while in a computer context, web means the world wide web.

Concept Reinforcement:

1. Explain further the difference between syntax and semantics. What additional capabilities would the semantic web have over the current web?

2. What are the benefits of standards in computer science and engineering?

3. What are the implications of the semantic web for privacy and security?

Section 3.14 – Future Human Computer Interaction Technologies

Section Objective:

- Analyze how future human computer interaction technologies may impact the science of computing

What are some trends in human computer interaction (HCI)?

Until recently the main modes by which humans interact with computers has been the keyboard together with a pointing device like a mouse, trackball, and touchpad. Some systems, especially used for customer applications as in Automatic Teller Machines, use touch sensitive screens. For detailed graphics, many use a graphics tablet along with a pen-like device. Many, if not all, of these are now available in wireless versions.

A photo of a Wacom pen tablet courtesy of Tobias Rutten.

Recently, other methods of HCI are becoming more common. Some tablet computers and PDAs use handwriting recognition, enabling users to scribble directly on a document displayed on the tablet using the supplied 'pen,' and save the scribbles or convert into text.

A technology used in some tablets and some PDAs is automatic completion in which the computer attempts to guess the remaining letters of a word you are entering from the first few letters. A simple version of this is also seen in other contexts. For example, some web browsers when typing in a URL. Here the software finds all recently entered URLs that could match the first few letters you are entering and displays these as choices. Some tablets and PDAs dispense with a hardware keyboard altogether, displaying instead a virtual keyboard when requested.

A picture of a phone with a virtual keyboard.

Voice recognition (VR) is also being used by many companies to save time of phone representatives. This is usually associated with automated voice response. Since these systems are being deployed by more and more organizations, it appears that companies find benefits but whether customers are uniformly fond of them is not clear. In this and other contexts, text-to-speech technologies are used in which the computer converts text into a humanoid voice. It is usually easy to tell that this speech is synthetic since it often lacks the pauses, inflections, accents, and other ways that humans are used to hearing, and which carries meaningful information beyond the words themselves.

Another interesting HCI technology that was recently deployed on the iPhone, is gesture recognition in which specific hand gestures (including finger tapping) are interpreted by the device as specific commands. The Nintendo WII uses motion sensing to duplicate the sensation, and visual response, of playing golf, tennis and other physical activities.

Some engineers have explored ways to transmit odors across the internet using a device that contains different aromatic chemicals that are mixed together into specific proportions to reproduce specific aromas. Others are now researching how to provide tactile sensations. In a somewhat related connection, the science of haptics is concerned with duplicating the pushing and pulling sensations felt by humans when doing specific mechanical tasks. There has been significant interest in this technology as a means of teaching surgery. The technology has been extended to include immersion in 3-D virtual reality for added realism.

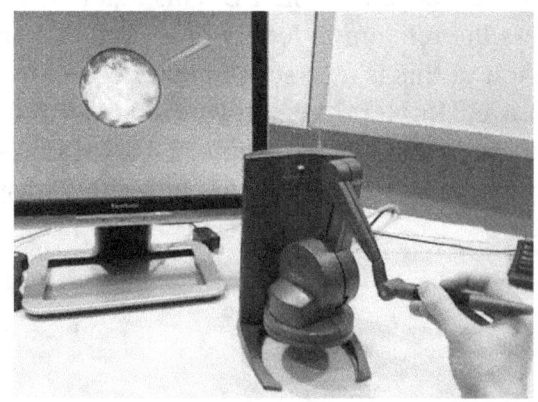

A picture of a haptic device.

The computer has also enabled development of Human patient simulators. These are life size mannequins (males, females, adults, children and infants) that display human physiology including breathing, temperature, heart sounds, pupil dilation, tongue thickening, and similar, in both normal and in disease states that can be programmed. Also, the mannequin can be treated with medication and will respond realistically.

The ultimate frontier of HCI may also be within reach: the control of a computer simply by thought. Recently a paraplegic individual, connected to brain wave sensors processed by special software was able to move a pointer on the screen by thinking about it. It is interesting to speculate on how soon this technology could become mainstream, and the consequences thereafter.

Concept Reinforcement:

1. Describe human computer interactions.

2. Why are handwriting and voice recognition so difficult for computers and so easy for humans?

3. Identify and explain at least 3 consequences of being able to control computers by thought.

Section 3.15 – Future Social Implications of Computing

Section Objective:

- Analyze how future social implications of information processing may impact the science of computing

What are some possible future social impacts of information processing?

There is little doubt that just in the past 15 years information processing, and communication technologies based on computing, have profoundly altered the way in which people live, work, and communicate. As computer scientists and engineers continue to innovate and make computing even more ubiquitous and pervasive, information processing will continue to have an impact on people. So far computing has had its greatest impact in the developed countries and on the higher-income segments of developing ones. However, efforts are being made by many to bring the benefits of computing to less-favored peoples. Laptops costing about $100 are being manufactured and put in the hands of underprivileged children. The cell phone is being used by fishermen in India to bypass middlemen and get more direct access, and hence better prices, for their catch. This has resulted in improved incomes for many.

On the technological side, it is clear that great progress is being made in many areas including robotics, intelligent agents, biomedical informatics. Advances in biomedical informatics could help grow better crops, help find better drugs, and manage patient care more effectively and cheaply. Telemedicine could help bring the best medical care even to remote regions. Multi-core processors may enable speedy solution of problems that are presently considered intractable. Computer displays that can be rolled up like a newspaper are already available in small form factors. Very likely, distance will not be an impediment to communicating odors and touch, just as sound and images can be transmitted interactively worldwide. Virtual reality and immersive 3-D environments will be the future of entertainment.

Of course, the above is only a mere fraction of the future applications that computing and communications technologies could enable. We must look to science fiction to provide more predictions.

Clearly, all these innovations will affect people's lives. Robots may perform household chores and take over many industrial processes. What does that do to the humans who work in those industries? The demise of industries such as steel and manufacturing caused tremendous social upheaval in many states of the US and in countries of Europe. Will the future progress in computing cause other industries to similarly collapse? If so which ones?

The information technologies of the future could also be used by criminals and terrorists to cause harm. The scientists and engineers that created the internet were idealists who believed that their innovations could be used for the benefit of mankind. They could not have foreseen that it would open up new ways to commit cyber-crimes such as identity theft and computer stalking, and lead to loss of privacy. Terrorists have been known to use the internet to deliver coded commands to their operatives and to spread their messages of hate. Will we be able to ensure that future communication and communications technologies will result in more benefit than harm? What kind of computing technologies can we develop for this purpose?

A photo of Sir Arthur Eddington.

A famous British astronomer, Sir Arthur Eddington, said (paraphrasing) that the universe is not only stranger than we imagine, it is probably stranger that we can imagine. Much the same can be said of the future of computing technologies, and its social implications: The future of computing is not only going to be more amazing than we imagine, it is probably going to be more amazing than we *can* imagine. I hope you will contribute to making it so!

Concept Reinforcement:

1. What kind of advances in computing and communication technologies do you expect in the next 25 years?

2. Pick one of the following areas: health, energy, transportation, politics. How will it be impacted by the advances you identified in #1?

3. Discuss the tension between legal and illegal uses of technologies and regulation of those technologies.

Appendix

Section 1.1

1. The geometric arrangement of stones and Aubrey holes in concentric circles. Evidence that smaller stones were periodically moved around and deposited in the Aubrey holes, possibly to represent numbers or other data.

2. These are 56 holes dug into the ground in a concentric circle within the outermost ring of stones.

3. (Answer not unique) If it can be conclusively determined that Stonehenge did indeed have a computational functionality it would show that computing has been an activity of humans dating back to thousands of years. Due to all the speculation and plausible theories in this regard, it has served as an inspiration to many.

Section 1.2

1. Mentally assign the decimal point between the 2nd and 3rd rods from the right. Start from the 6th rod from the right, move 2 earth beads to the center beam. On the 5th rod from right move one heaven bead and one earth bead to the center beam. On the 4th rod from right move one heaven bead to the center beam. On the 3rd from right move one heaven bead and 3 earth beads to the center beam. On the 2nd rod from right move 3 earth beads to the center beam and finally 2 earth beads to the center beam in the rightmost rod.

2. In the 6th rod from the right move one earth bead to the beam. In the 5th rod move another earth bead towards the beam and one heaven bead away from the beam. In the 4th rod move two earth beads to the center beam. In the 3rd rod move another earth bead to the center beam. In the 2nd rod move one heaven bead to the center beam and two earth beads away from the center beam. In the 1st rod move another earth bead to the center beam. Now read off 3289.63.

3. Not directly since there is no negative sign. Complementary numbers (Chap. 1.3) are used.

Section 1.3

1. 30567

2. $734 + 734 + \ldots + 734$ (49 additions).

3. The Pascaline computer is a mechanical arrangement of gears, levers, and sprocketed wheels that could perform arithmetical calculations. Designed primarily to perform additions it could be adapted, with some help from the operator to subtract, multiply and divide. It showed that mechanical devices could perform arithmetic and inspired several other inventors to improve the design and produce reliable mechanical calculators.

Section 1.4

1. Mechanical computers consist of physical moving parts that are subject to wear and tear, friction, mechanical breakdown, and heat generation. The moving parts typically require lots of energy to drive them and are much larger and slower than electronic devices.

2. The DE was mainly designed to compute values of polynomials. In other words, it performed essentially only one fixed type of computation. The AE, in theory, could perform any computation, including execution of conditional (if-then-else) that could be encoded onto the punched cards.

Section 1.5

1. Previous attempts at collecting statistical data were subject to substantial operator error in transferring data from the census-takers forms to the statistical tables and in adding up the counts into various categories. .Humans were also slow at performing these tasks and their work had to be double-checked often. The Tabulating Machine eliminated most of these errors by automating the entire process using electromechanical machines.

2. The punched card contained rows and columns. Specific rows, or sets of rows corresponded to categories of data such as age, gender, occupation and so on. The keypunch operator entered data from the census-takers sheets into these cards using typewriter keys. This machine punched holes in the cards. Thus the punched cards served as a data representation that facilitated entry of the information into the electromechanical tabulating machine.

Section 1.6

1. Mathematically, any number can be represented in binary form. Scientists and engineers have invented and perfected technologies based on electromagnetic components that can reliably be in one of two states at any given time. These components serve as the basic building blocks for the storage of numbers and alphabetic characters in modern computers.

2. ASCII standards use one byte (eight bits) to represent up to 256 distinct symbols. By associating numbers, letters and special characters with specific combinations, the ASCII representation provides a common standard by which alphanumeric characters can be represented within computers.

3. A device that can be in more than 2 states can represent the same number as a binary device using less space. For example, a single device that could be in 8 states can represent any number from 0 to 7 with just one unit. On the other hand, 3 binary units are needed to represent the numbers 0 to 7. Thus, devices that can store 3 or more states can store more information using lesser numbers of components. This could lead to more powerful computers capable of storing and manipulating much more data than present-day computers.

Section 1.7

1. The drum memory of the Mark 1 corresponds to the rigid (hard) disks in modern computers.

2. The Williams-Kilburn tubes functioned as Random Access Memory, enabling programs and data to be stored temporarily for processing by the CPU. Intermediate results were also written and retrieved into these tubes by the CPU.

3. Reconfiguring hardware, accomplished by humans throwing switches and reconnecting internal cables is an inherently tedious and slow process. Debugging (fixing errors) in a computation could eat up lots of time, running into days. The stored program computer overcomes all these limitations and provides a way to make the computer hardware perform practically any computation imaginable and to debug it in comparatively much less time.

Section 1.8

1. Random Access Memory. In a modern computer programs and data are first loaded into RAM and then processed by the CPU.

2. The Turing Machine is an abstract model of computing that is powerful enough to represent any computation.

3. The action table contains instructions that, depending on the current state of the machine (including the symbol just read from the tape), say which direction the tape is to be moved, whether to read or write from the tape, and what symbol (if any) to write. In this way it alters the state of the machine.

Section 1.9

1. Unlike previous computers, the ENIAC was not designed specifically to perform any one type or types of calculations. It was theoretically capable of doing anything that could conceivably be regarded as computing. However, because it was programmed by humans throwing switches and re-routing and reconnecting internal wiring, as a practical matter it was very difficult to 'write' and debug complex programs.

2. Early general purpose computers were 'programmed' by mechanical reconfiguration of switches and wiring by humans. In effect, the stored program architecture enabled the computer to be programmed without any such limitations and thus enabled programmers to write and debug easily very complex computations.

Section 1.10

1. Without the IC the microprocessor could not have existed in the current form. The IC enabled several orders of magnitude of miniaturization of electronic components like the transistor, capacitor, diodes and so on. It eliminated the need to do wiring between these components. All of these benefits of the IC, and others, made the microprocessor possible.

2. Some of the multiple consequences of Moore's Law are as follows. The number of transistors on the microprocessor doubles about once every two years. The computing performance increases while the cost per transistor decreases However, reliability could decrease because the transistor density (number of transistors per sq cm) increases rapidly. Power consumption and heat build-up also increase.

3. Excessive heat buildup can damage the microprocessor and cause it to fail.

Section 1.11

1. The CPU processes instructions in a stream of 1s and 0s called Machine language. However, this is very hard for humans to use and develop software with. PLs present an English-like set of words and syntax that make it much easier for humans to write complex software.

2. Iteration, branching.

3. (More than one answer possible). Words and sentences in natural languages can have multiple meanings that can be disambiguated only by context and other indicators. For example the word 'or' can be either exclusive or inclusive. The same word can have one meaning in England and another in the USA. Writing a compiler to understand natural languages and convert into a completely unambiguous form suitable for processing by a CPU is an extremely difficult task that has not yet been accomplished. Therefore, most programming languages are only English-like and not full English. Current programming languages follow very rigid rules of syntax (unlike natural languages) and typically allow only unique meanings of the words, or very few choices that can easily be clarified by the immediate context.

Section 1.12

1. (Answer not unique) PCs don't have to be shared with potentially hundreds of other persons, providing greater privacy and freedom of use. PCs can easily be customized even at the hardware level to the user's needs.

2. (Answer not unique). From the perspective of hardware performance, it is possible that future cell phones could match that of today's laptops. Currently many tablet computers can have keyboards as accessories, making them function like notebook computers.

Section 1.13

1. In circuit switching a physically continuous path is established between the communicating entities and the data are sent in a stream through this circuit. In packet switching the data are broken up into discrete packets and each packet is sent from the server to several intermediate routing stations before it reaches the intended destination.

2. Each packet in a message is sent to several intermediate locations. The routing tables in each such location could have multiple forwarding addresses as the next step en route to the final destination. The choice of a particular one can depend on traffic conditions and other factors.

Section 1.14

1. The internet is a vast worldwide collection of networked computers. The world wide web is a subset that supports and executes data sharing protocols and languages such as HTTP, HTML, and others.

2. Domain Name servers provide the translation between English-like URLS like www.uthouston.edu and the corresponding IP addresses.

3. The HyperText Transfer Protocol is the fundamental standard by which inter-linked documents located within web pages are accessed. Using a web browser, a user makes a request for a web page using the http format. This is parsed, using rules based on the http protocol by a responding web server and the document, is supplied to the requester.

Section 1.15

1. Complex and feature-rich web sites need to be created by powerful compiled programming languages such as C++. Two tier systems using just JavaScript and ASP (Active Sever pages) are insufficient to create the advanced functionality expected in the web these days.

2. The DBMS manages accesses to the underlying database of the web site. It accepts request for data and converts them into queries and database logic, taking into account security considerations, and returns the information to the requesting layer.

3. The Active Server pages layer, among other functionality, provides a rich set of user interface objects like check boxes, radio buttons etc on the web page. It then hands over the user request from these objects to the layer responsible for processing these requests. The ASP layer also redraws the web page to display the results of these queries. Thus ASP supports dynamic web pages.

The Science of Computing Answer Key Unit 2

Section 2.1

1. Each time Step 2 is executed one number is set aside from the input list to the destination list. Therefore, after N executions of step 2 the original list will be empty. According to the termination rule (Step 4) the algorithm will stop.

2. One way is to create an abstract ordering of letters in which A is the least, B is the second least and Z is the maximum. Next, a 3 letter word can be ordered so that the left-most letter is the most significant (something like the 100s place in a 3 digit number) and the right-most has the least significance. For example, DOG is "greater" than CAT. The sort algorithm given in the Section can be used with this way of ordering 3-letter words.

3. This is not an algorithm since no termination (stopping) rule is specified. An example of such a rule would be "Mix well and bake at 415 degrees for 45 minutes".

Section 2.2

1. (Answer not unique) Suppose that the name for the numeral data type is INT and that for the alphabetic character is CHAR. Suppose also that in this PL the word Array is used to describe a string of data items.
    Then, a possible data structure looks like this:
    DefineDataStructure TelephoneBookEntry
    FirstName CHAR(20)
    LastName Array CHAR(40)
    TelephoneNum INT(10)
    End TelephoneBookEntry
    Here, Array Char(20) indicates a string of at most 20 characters.

2. (Answers not unique) Some methods that are appropriate to RegularPolygons are "Locate Centroid", "Rotate polygon 45 degrees around centroid", "Fill up a square of side 10 meters (for example) with hexagons of side 5 inches (for example)". An operation that is not appropriate could be "Calculate volume of RegularPolygon".

Section 2.3

1. Design goals can drive engineers to develop new technologies and invent new methods. For example if given the task of building a storage device capable of 10 Gb capacity in a cube not more than half a cubic inch volume engineers would explore very high density magnetic or Flash storage. The current goal of reducing carbon emission drastically over the next 20 years is causing engineers to develop better car batteries.

2. Industry standards have many functions. One important one is to enable multiple developers and organizations to integrate their products by following standards while developing their products. For example, because consumer electricity outlets in the USA are set at a standard of 110V, 50 Hz, manufacturers of systems units, computer displays, TVs etc can be sure their components will work together by designing the electronics to accept electricity at 110V and 50 Hz. A more complex example is described in the Section.

3. Standards can provide a target for future technologies to achieve. For example, the wireless standards like 802.11b, 802.11g, and so on were set at a time when the technologies did not really exist but were deemed to be feasible by experts.

Section 2.4

1. Some advantages (there are likely others) are: a) Easy search using complex criteria; b) Easy edit and update of the material; c) It is cheap and easy to make as many copies as needed; d) It is easy to distribute the material widely using email, web and similar electronic means.

2. One problem with disk storage is that each format requires a specialized reader. If the reader technology becomes obsolete then disks written in that format can become unreadable. For example, it is very hard to find readers of 8" and 5.25" floppy disk media these days.

3. Here's a simple relational table for this purpose.

Field Name (Data item)	Data Type	Description
AuthorLN (Primary Key)	Text	Last name of Author. Will be used as primary key for this database
AuthorFN	Text	First name of Author
Title	Text	Title of Book
NumPages	Numeric	Number of pages in the book
Language	Text	Language book is written in
StartDate	Date (mmddyyyy)	Date I started reading
EndDate	Date (mmddyyyy)	Date I completed reading it
Finished?	Boolean (True or False)	True if I finished reading it, False else
Comments	Text	My comments on the book

Section 2.5

1. Many potential applications exist. High resolution high format (like IMAX) computer graphics/animation; mining very large databases including the world wide web; highly accurate weather forecasting.

2. (Answer not unique) Some concurrent activities performed by the brain include consciousness, response to external auditory and visual stimuli, motor activity, monitoring physical activities of the body such as respiration, digestion, maintenance of body temperature and many others.

3. For example consider two computations P1 and P2. If the input data to P2 depends on the output data of P1 then P2 must wait until P1 is completed. Such computations are necessarily serial. Example, a check must clear at the issuing bank before the amount can be finally added to the target (deposit) account.

Section 2.6

1. Three such attributes (there are others) perception, consciousness, context/ situational awareness.

2. Number crunching usually consists of the application of arithmetic formulae in repetitive ways. There is no active opponent whose intention is to prevent the computation from occurring. Playing chess requires the ability to recognize current and future patterns, anticipate the opponent"s response several steps in advance, constantly searching for strategies and other complex cognition.

3. Many repetitive activities performed by humans could be aided by AI. Some of these are fingerprint identification, web searching, data mining, medical decision support, driving a vehicle and others.

Section 2.7

1. Systems programming is usually concerned with tasks that are required to make the computer and associated systems function. Examples include managing the disk subsystem, automatically transferring programs and data between CPU, RAM, disk, and similar. Applications programs are the ones that humans directly invoke to perform activities related to work or entertainment. Word processing, running spreadsheets, watching movies etc are examples of applications programs.

2. One function of the Operating System is to manage the interface between the hardware and the applications program. Once installed on a particular hardware configuration the OS receives commands from OS-compatible applications and translates those into the low-level details corresponding to the particular hardware configuration.

3. A multi-tasking OS can have more than one application executing at any given time. A multi-user OS allows multiple users to be accessing the system simultaneously. A multi-tasking OS is not necessarily a multi-user OS.

Section 2.8

1. The clock is used to regulate the flow of instructions are processed and also to help synchronize the data flow between various computer components.

2. The final performance of a computer is dependent on multiple factors such as the speed of the bus, the speed of data access in the disk subsystem, whether caching is provided, video refresh rates, and many others. The clock speed of the CPU is only one component of the overall system.

3. The function of the bus is to transfer data from system components such as disks, I/O subsystem, video cards etc and the CPU.

Section 2.9

1. Each pixel consists of three-color components, for example, Red Green and Blue. By controlling the brightness of each component the pixel can be made to display different colors. Each combination of bits in a 24-bit display can specify one combination of color brightness. The number of possible combinations of bits in a 24 bit display is $2^{24} = 16,777,216$.

2. (Answer not unique) The techniques of computer graphics enable display of higher resolution, realistic and complex images, including 3-D. All of these can contribute to a richer more satisfying human computer interface.

Section 2.10

1. $30 \times 2 \times 60 \times 60 = 216{,}000$

2. In a feature film designed to be projected at high resolution on a large screen the system needs to calculate intricate combinations of graphics objects including lighting, shading, colors, brightness, transparency, opacity, and a host of other visual details. All of these result in complex, time-consuming computations.

3. (Answer not unique) CGA can be used in contexts like scientific visualization, medical simulations, creating walkthroughs within complex habitations such as buildings and space habitations.

Section 2.11

1. A security model describes the various categories of users of a system and the kinds of access to system functionalities provided to them.

2. A strong password uses longer combinations of letters, numbers and special characters than weak ones. Strong password systems do not allow the use of common words and easily guessed ones such as the user"s name and other personal details. Further, strong passwords systems require the user to change the password at regular intervals. All of these features make strong passwords harder than weak ones to crack.

3. Many people store personal information such as access codes to bank accounts, cookies to facilitate login into personal email system, address books containing contact information for friends. Some have been known to scan and store financial data such as bank statements, social security cards, driver's licenses and similar information of great interest to identity thieves.

Section 2.12

1. (Answer not unique). Many people regard google.com to have a good user interface. Information is presented in a clean, unambiguous manner and the functionality is clear.

2. Extensibility is concerned with being able to easily add new features and functionality to software. Scalability has to do with the software being able to provide good response times and good performance even when the number of simultaneous users, or the amount of information it is required to process, increases greatly.

3. Software written for public use has to provide an interface that is easy and intuitive to use for persons who may have very little previous knowledge of its intent and functionality. If data entry is required it must be very clear what kinds of data are requested. Error messages must be provided to help the user overcome any mistakes. Navigation must be clear and unambiguous.

When writing software for personal use most people are very aware of its functionality, limitations, types of allowable data and other characteristics. There is no need to build the features and user-interface items described in the previous paragraph.

Section 2.13

1. Distributed computing enables people to break up large computing tasks into smaller pieces that can be processed simultaneously on the various computers in the network.

2. The statement expresses the view that computing is performed across the entire network of computers rather than just one.

3. A repeater takes a weak signal as input and re-transmits it at higher strength. It is needed because electronic signals tend to decrease in strength (attenuate) as they traverse long distances in a network.

Section 2.14

1. Hint for this question and next. Is the functionality of the web site or software clear to lay users? Is navigation intuitive and unambiguous? Is it clear what data are requested and are clear error message provided if the user inputs incorrect data?

3. Garish colors and loud noises may be appropriate for certain types of games and target audiences. However, such may not be appropriate for a website for the elderly or those that are targeted to patients with certain kinds of neurological conditions.

Section 2.15

1. (Answer not unique) Access to instant information via the web; ability to store and analyze vast quantities of data; instant communications via email, instant messaging.

2. (Answer not unique) Potential loss of privacy, cyber-harassment/stalking. Certain industries such as travel agencies have suffered losses and shrinkage as sophisticated web sites perform their activities.

3. (Answer not unique) Cell phones are well on their way to becoming ubiquitous computing/communications devices. They have the potential to enable people to reach others anywhere anyplace. The internet, web sites, email could be available on most if not all cell phones. Health workers and laypersons could access medical assistance no matter where they are located. Getting lost may be a thing of the past as web-based maps become available instantly anywhere. The possibilities, both good and ill, are limitless.

The Science of Computing Answer Key Unit 3

Section 3.1

1. (Answer not unique). Imaging (including medical imaging such as MRIs), technologies to store vast quantities of data cheaply, and explosive growth of the world wide web.

2. $O(N^2)$ is faster because the function N^2 increases at a much lower rate than 2^N.

3. A generic algorithm produces multiple candidate solutions to a problem then applies a 'fitness' function to select the best one among them.

Section 3.2

1. Hint: Does this language allow you to create generalized objects, easily manipulate strings of alphanumeric characters, have a good extension of if-then-else to handle multiple choices?

2. (Answer not unique). Support for a special sensor object to handle input from environmental sensors giving information about location, presence of walls, stairs, carpets, dust, dirt.

3. Imperative programming is based on statements that command the processor to perform specific actions such as ADD, READ, WRITE etc. Declarative programming is used to describe data sets, documents, web pages and similar.

Section 3.3

1. (Answer not unique). With respect to hardware the computer components have to be designed in such a way as not to interfere with user comfort. Wireless communications to displays, printers and audio outputs are needed.

2. (Answer not unique). The main challenge is to present large amounts of visual content such as web pages and emails in a small screen. Similarly, input of text data like emails or URLs on small devices can be challenging.

3. (Answer not unique). This depends on the functionality desired by the consumer. For intense game playing very fast and realistic displays, quick response times, high sound fidelity, powerful processors and similar. Other users may desire highly portable and mobile machines with integrated communications. Intuitive, easy to use software and human-computer interface is desired by all. Voice command and handwriting recognition is becoming increasingly desirable.

Section 3.4

1. (Answer not unique). Object Oriented databases, Image databases. Very large databases containing heterogeneous data (images, audio).

2. Most programming languages today are object-oriented. However, data are typically stored in a relational format. This means that additional programming has to be done to convert the relational data into the objects processed by programming languages. Object-oriented databases aim to store data in the form of objects that are convenient and meaningful to application programmers interfacing with the database.

Section 3.5

1. Greater data compression would be possible resulting in faster communication speeds.

2. Storage devices with vastly greater capacity can be developed. Computations could be performed without having to first convert into binary and then back again. Advanced pattern recognition based on analog values, not digital ones, could be performed.

Section 3.6

1. Narrow AI is focused on specific tasks like handwriting or speech recognition. AGI is concerned with generalized intelligence including consciousness, perception, self-awareness and similar.

2. To train a computer how to perform specific tasks. This can be done in a supervised or unsupervised way. In the former, a human explicitly advises the computer when it has made correct or incorrect choices.

3. Grammar checking has elements that would be considered AI, such as recognition of context, and the importance of semantics (meaning).

Section 3.7

1. (Answer not unique). 3-D interfaces can provide a richer, more intuitive experience to a user. In real-life most objects such as books and rooms are 3-D, so a 3-D user interface can provide visual metaphors that are more natural and easily understood.

2. Real time computing includes tasks that must be completed according to specific time constraints. For example, a system designed to detect alarming variations in a patients heart rate must be able to provide alerts to caregivers within seconds of the event occurring.

3. Mobile computing is concerned with portable devices such as cell phones, and personal digital assistants. In both data and voice communication contexts, the system must be able to provide continuous, uninterrupted access even though the user may be walking through a building, or driving at high speed down a highway.

Section 3.8

1. Sending bulk emails can be parallelized because transmitting email to any person on the list does not have to wait on sending email to any other.

2. Retrieving/entering an email address into the To field, and actually sending it out cannot be parallelized. The first operation must occur before the second.

3. The memory wall refers to slow data transfer from memory to/from CPU relative to the speed of the CPU itself. If the CPU is forced to wait for data from memory then it cannot process data as fast as its theoretical capability.

Section 3.9

1. A voxel is a volume element existing in 3-D space. A pixel is a picture element existing in 2-D.

2. (Answer not unique) 3-D games, medical imaging, immersive virtual reality.

Section 3.10

1. (Answer not unique). Underlying hard tissue (bones), body structures, facial details including shapes of skull, eyes, mouth, nose, cheekbones. Hair movement.

2. Example: Consider a ride film of white-water rafting. Challenges will include developing the types of motion like jolting, scraping on racks, being flung into the water, going over waterfalls. Simulating water, movement, spray, surf, scenery going by at various speeds etc.

Section 3.11

1. (Answer not unique) Copying an infected file from a floppy disk or flash disk. Database servers have been compromised by 'SQL Injection' attacks in which a database query contains special characters and processing of this query led to the attacker being able to perform malicious actions.

2. (Answer not unique). Users leaving password information in easily accessible locations, sharing passwords with others even when explicitly forbidden to do so by institutional rules.

3. Example criteria: Email from unknown sender. Subject line with offer of money or "cheap drugs". Request for personal information in mail body.

Section 3.12

1. Advantages: Each person can check the others work and be a resource for ideas and 'how to' questions. Disadvantages: Personality and emotional conflicts could arise to prevent the pair from being productive.

2. (Answer not unique) The different platforms may not all support some essential features such as being able to play audio/video. Since the screen sizes range from very large to very small it may not be possible to provide consistent screens. Certain platforms may have a full keyboard/mouse while others may not.

Section 3.13

1. Syntax is concerned with the proper formation of symbols in a language. For example, in English the letter 'q' is almost always followed by the letter 'u'. Correct spelling of words is also a concern of syntax. On the other hand semantics is concerned with the abstractions, consequences, and meanings of words, phrases and sentences.

   The semantic web could allow knowledge to be more easily organized and searched for in terms of higher level concepts such as "snow-covered mountains", "luxury properties on islands" and similar. Searches based on these words as keywords currently result in lots of irrelevant data. Semantic searches can potentially be more directed and meaningful.

2. Standards enable different groups such as hardware, software, and communications engineers, to develop devices that meet performance and functional goals and enable the devices to work together. Multiple manufacturers can independently design and build their own versions of a product designed for the same goal. For example, you can buy a wireless modem from any number of manufacturers for the same standard, e.g., 802.11b, and expect similar performance from all.

3. The semantic web can potentially enable searches based on more meaningful and broad criteria than keyword search. This could enable malicious individuals to more easily target and gain information about large groups of people by, eg, racial or religious, or financial semantic criteria.

Section 3.14

1. Both of these activities are forms of pattern recognition, akin to facial recognition. Human brains have the intrinsic capability to simultaneously look for, process, and recognize the multiple characteristics comprising speech and handwriting. However, computers are essentially serial devices that use sequential algorithms based on mathematical and logical programming. Such kinds of reasoning are very hard to optimize for facial, handwriting and speech recognition.

2. (Answer not unique) Physically impaired people could enjoy the benefits of computing; input devices like keyboards could become obsolete; computer output could become available without the need to see it in a display.

Section 3.15

1. (Answer not unique) Multi-core (up to 100 cores) processors will become cheap and ubiquitous. Wireless data communication will become 10 million times faster.

2. (Answer not unique). Health: physicians will be able to almost instantly retrieve and apply algorithms to analyze complete information about a patient including lab tests, imaging, clinical history. This information will be made available no matter where on earth (or space) the patient is located. Latest information on available treatments will be available immediately.